KENTUCKY'S EVERYDAY
HEROES FOR KIDS

This Book is
from the Frie
the Oldham C
Library

Kentucky's Everyday Heroes
for Kids

Ordinary People
Doing Extraordinary Stuff

By Steve Flairty

Illustrated by Rita DeLozier-Abshear
Edited by Michael Embry

WIND PUBLICATIONS

International Standard Book Number 978-1-936138-51-7
Library of Congress Control Number 2012938398

First edition

Dedicated to Morgan Alexander,

friend and walkin' buddy ...

and always a good sport.

Contents

Acknowledgements 1

Introduction 5

Kasey Fields 9

Jamie Vaught 12

Mike Howard 17

Bear Stories 21

    Dick and Ardi Wilson 21

    Taelor Martin 23

    Landen Speck & Briana Stout 25

Charles Whitaker 28

Jody Keeley 32

Tim Farmer 37

Judy Hensley 42

Dr. George Wright 47

Grace Harvey 52

Brian Huybers 55

Mary Lou Boal 60

Kendall Harvey 65

Fanestia Massey 69

Russell Vassallo 74

Doug and Shelia Bray 79

Bennie Doggett 85

Roy Pullam 89

Darlene Snyder 94

Jim Lyon, Sr. 98

Dale Faughn 102

Don Rose 108

Kevin Gunderson 112

Bill Gordon 116

Acknowledgements

I am grateful to the hundreds of people, mostly youngsters, who helped make *Kentucky's Everyday Heroes for Kids* a reality.

Thanks again to my tireless and skillful editor, Michael Embry, who has patiently worked with me on three books. I'm excited and appreciative, also, about talented illustrator Rita DeLozier-Abshear. Rita has brought a graphically fun and easy touch to the heroes—and I thank publisher Charlie Hughes for suggesting we do so.

Many thanks go to the fourth and fifth grade students at Nicholasville, Wilmore and Brookside Elementary Schools in Jessamine County. I asked the students to help me write a book that Kentucky kids their age could read, be inspired by, and enjoy. They did help, and participated in the process over about a six-month period.

Students read carefully over a selective sampling of the stories and were instructed to be honest in their thoughts and suggestions. They wrote lots of comments and asked many pertinent questions about the text. Students pointed out what they considered awkward sentences, "too hard" words, and even found spelling errors; they also let me know the parts they really liked. What a nice field testing experience it was for me—and hopefully them, too. Besides, who is better equipped to provide feedback than the audience for whom the book is intended to reach?

One major, and, I believe, positive change to the writing of the book came from the students' suggestion to call our heroes by their first names. "It's more personal," several stated. As I tried that idea, I liked it, too. It made the stories sound more real, less like reading a newspaper—and even more fun to write. The students nudged me towards changing a lot of "big words" to more simple ones they could easily understand … and I liked that idea, too. Truly, I leaned on, and am thankful for, the important part these Jessamine County students played in making *Kentucky's Everyday Heroes for Kids* ready for all to read.

Others, in various ways, played roles in moving the project along: Trevor Scott, Suzanne Isaacs, Tracy Gatliff, Kim Leet, Mike Snyder, Carl Nelson, Jill Snyder, Joe Gabriel, and Eric Fruge encouraged me. Fifth grade teacher Connie Jean Royse graciously read story drafts in order to check for student readability issues. Noted Kentucky children's author, Marcia Thornton Jones, wrote a kind testimonial for the back cover, and I'm humbled. As always, my morning coffee and daily writing preparation usually started at the local Panera Bread; I don't know what I'd do without that gentle buzz toward productive work.

A special note of thanks goes to the everyday heroes previously profiled in the first two volumes of *Kentucky's Everyday Heroes*. The ones chosen from the regular series for this kids' volume were happy to have their stories rewritten in a more "youth friendly" way, and it is my hope that their examples will inspire an even greater audience going forward.

For those who have read all the *Heroes* series, along with the Tim Farmer biography—my first book—thanks greatly for your interest. Hope you have been uplifted.

Finally, I'm so blessed and thankful for the commonwealth of Kentucky, a place that supplies me with a never-ending source of positive stories to share. My aim, as always, is to shine light on the best attributes the Bluegrass state has … its everyday heroes.

Introduction

In elementary school, I spent many happy times in the library and duplicating room at Grants Lick Elementary School searching for just the right book, usually a biography. I liked non-fiction, and I wanted to read about historical persons who seemed to be bigger than life itself—and hoped that this naïve little boy could be "as big" someday, too.

The room was so small that my teacher would allow only a few students at a time to leave the regular classroom to browse the shelves, and only for a short while so that every class member could get a turn. In this "library closet," as my classmate Billie Jo Chaplin called it, I'd sprawl down on the floor to get a good look at the bottom shelf where the American biography series' titles sat upright, showing on the spines stars like Kit Carson, Charles Lindbergh, Amelia Earhart and many of our presidents. Over time, I read most of them; I especially liked the ones of Kentuckians, including Abraham Lincoln, Daniel Boone and Henry Clay. Each of them had courage, was wise, and they made my state look good. I looked at the people in those books as my personal heroes—almost as much as my favorite basketball players on the Kentucky Wildcats. And *that* was sure saying a lot!

As I grew older, I continued to choose famous heroic figures as an important part of what I read, but I also began to notice special people in my community as they lived out their daily lives right in front of me. Some were overcomers, born poor or with physical challenges. Some simply were encouragers or helpers.

Those individuals were not "famous" in the way of those books I read, but they were shining stars in my eyes. They lived quiet, caring and courageous lives, and folks around my community surely looked up to them. My Aunt Thelma, for example, was always taking food to the sick or visiting lonely senior citizens at nursing homes. Two different families often drove ten miles out of their way to take me to church. My Little League baseball manager didn't curse and seldom threw a temper tantrum. And despite the fact I wasn't good enough to play much, he always made me feel special by bragging on my good fielding as I never figured out how to hit the ball. Later, when I graduated from college and took a teaching job in Winchester at a very low salary, George Schnorr took a day out of his life and helped me find an affordable apartment. There were many more individuals like the ones mentioned, and you, the reader, likely can think of special persons in your life, too.

Many decades later, I am thankful for the difference these local citizens made in me as a youngster lacking in confidence and needing some solid, trustworthy guidance. These were my friends, fellow Kentuckians and everyday heroes.

Today, I seek to honor and shine light on such individuals. A sense of thankfulness and excitement inspires me to devote much of my time these days to interviewing like persons ... now, as author of the *Kentucky's Everyday Heroes* book series.

I've had the opportunity to discuss the series on statewide TV and many radio stations. With all the positive feedback, however, it is clear to me that an important audience for the books, elementary students, has not been served most fully. Our young people need good role models, especially ones outside of the narrow realm of sports "heroes."

I decided to do something to improve the situation.

As a retired elementary teacher who still teaches part-time, I enjoy telling a selection of the dozens of published stories to classes. The stories told orally draw much interest, but the actual book reading level for many elementary students is difficult, presenting an obstacle to their embracing the books as checkout material.

This young people's version of the series, I hope, will go a long way to address that concern.

In offering *Kentucky's Everyday Heroes for Kids*, my hope is that elementary students, especially intermediate readers, will be drawn to an easy-to-read style that captures their imaginations, and, yes, even inspires them to do what I like to call "greater works of character."

Kids includes an inviting, light-hearted assortment of sketch art images of the heroes, drawn by talented illustrator, Rita DeLozier-Abshear. Most of the stories are adapted from both volumes one and two of *Kentucky's Everyday Heroes,* and included are a number of new accounts of younger people who have performed admirable acts, often despite difficult odds.

In summary, I want *Kentucky's Everyday Heroes for Kids* to be a good and lasting way to connect with inspiration with our state's most precious resource—children. For them, I'm hoping it will be a frequent choice to check out of their own library closet!

Kasey Fields

Changing the World One Shoe at a Time

Kasey Fields has loads of talent and energy just waiting to be used to improve the lives of others. Lexington's School for the Creative and Performing Arts, where Kasey attends, helped her harness those traits into showing some remarkable leadership when she was a sixth-grader. The school, along with her highly supportive parents, produced a real winner of a kid!

Kasey said she was inspired by one of her teachers, Melanie Stivers, "to find ways I could change our world for the better." She began searching for ideas, but couldn't seem to settle on one.

"I kept coming back to wanting to focus on education, exercise, and our environment," Kasey continued. "Then one Sunday at church during announcements, a volunteer came up to talk about Soles 4 Souls, an organization that collects gently used shoes for needy people worldwide. I learned that there are people in other countries who can't even go to school if they don't have shoes. That's devastating. I decided I wanted to work and fix this problem."

Kasey decided to hold a five-kilometer race and asked participants to donate one or more pairs of gently used shoes as a registration fee. With that plan, she could both gather shoes to help others and promote exercise.

However, it was not easy to bring the event to a successful completion. First, she had to find a location. When she did, there were costs, rules, and even an insurance policy to buy. That took about two months. She had to get about a dozen volunteers to help on the day of the event. In the weeks and days leading up to the event, Kasey was nearly overwhelmed by the "adult" responsibilities she had in preparing for her project of compassion, but she kept her focus on finding good advice—which she did— and the fact that she was helping "change our world for the better."

Kasey will never forget the special Soles 4 Souls day as it unfolded on May 23, 2011. "I was really excited and nervous, too," she said. "It turned out to be one of the most memorable days of my life! One hundred and forty-two people raced and spectators came to show support and donate shoes. By the end of the day, I had collected almost eight hundred pairs of shoes! The next day my team boxed and shipped the shoes to a distribution center. From there, the shoes I'd helped to collect were shipped to people all around the world. I learned my shipment went to Haiti and Africa."

Ms. Stivers, her teacher, could barely contain her enthusiasm when talking about her energetic and committed pupil.

"She was leading a large effort, with many moving parts and a whole team of volunteers acting under her supervision. In addition to her studies, speech team, swimming, dancing, and running, Kasey volunteers countless hours and incredibly positive energy … (and) Kasey wants to use her unique talents and passion to make a positive contribution to her community and to our world."

Because of her work, largely for the shoe project, Kasey was recently awarded the Nicholas Green Distinguished Student Award given for a student who "has not only achieved in academics, leadership or the arts but also contributed to the community at a level beyond his or her age expectations."

Kasey's mother, Kathy Fields, remarked, "Once Kasey gets it in her mind she wants to do something, she is very persistent about it. She has an 'anything's possible' outlook which, I think, helps people jump on board with her ideas."

In a world that is full of challenges, it's refreshing to see a youngster "fill the shoes" of ones usually much older than her through her positive leadership in her community.

On that count, Kasey Fields is off and running!

Jamie Vaught

Sports Passion Helps Beat Hearing Limitations

For as long as he can remember, Jamie Vaught has been "Crazy about the Cats."

He has even written four books about those Cats, who are known to those who don't live in the state as the University of Kentucky Wildcats basketball program. In fact, the love Jamie feels for his favorite team, along with many sports, may be one of the biggest reasons for the way he overcame a difficult physical hardship to become a successful author, columnist and college professor.

Jamie was born in 1956 as a premature baby in Somerset, a small town in southern Kentucky not far from the Lake Cumberland park area. His parents quickly realized that little Jamie had something about him that didn't seem right. "When I was about two, my parents said I was real grouchy, fussy and did not respond to talking," Jamie said.

After Jamie's parents were told by doctors he was "severely hard of hearing," the family made a plan they thought would be best for his future well-being. A very important part of the plan was to decide where he would go to school. They considered the

Kentucky School for the Deaf in Danville, a school for students with hearing impairments—and a place where he could also live. But a very small school in Science Hill, near Somerset, offered to work closely with the family to help with Jamie's special needs. By going to Science Hill, he'd get a good education and stay at home, too.

Life became an adventure for Jamie and the ones who loved him. "I became the family project," he said with a grin, "and my mother and grandmother would work with me almost every night. My sister was sixteen years older and got married at eighteen, so she couldn't help on a regular basis."

So with his family's support, his good mind and a desire to work hard, Jamie became a very good student—all the way through college at the University of Kentucky, where he received two degrees. His success was quite surprising to some. "The doctors told my mother I would always be in the bottom third of my classes," said Jamie, "but I was in the top third."

It didn't come easy, though, especially in college. "I had note-takers, some good, some bad," he said. "There were also some teachers who had a beard, which made it hard to lip read."

Despite the difficulties, he finished college with almost an A– average in accounting, a difficult major. It's interesting to note that accounting was recommended for him, said Jamie, because "they said I wouldn't have to be around other people very much."

While at UK, Jamie joined the school's newspaper, the *Kentucky Kernel*. He was named the sports editor and could now report on his beloved Wildcats, whether it was the basketball, football or other teams at the school. He was in "Blue Heaven" and he knew it, but that was only a start for what came later in 1981.

Jamie received a position as a columnist for Oscar Combs's *Cats' Pause* weekly, a very popular newspaper read by thousands around the state. Despite having a severe hearing impairment, Jamie Vaught showed he could communicate to a sizeable audience—readers that looked forward every week to reading his thoughts about the Wildcats. He worked for Cats' Pause for thirteen years, and his writing got better and better.

Jamie met a lot of people in Kentucky sports who liked and trusted him. That popularity proved very important as he started writing his first book. He interviewed dozens of people about the Kentucky basketball program, and in 1991, he published his first book, *Crazy about the Cats*. It was a hit, selling about eleven thousand copies. He later wrote three more books on the subject, and they also sold well. Not bad for a person who doctors said would always be in the bottom third of his classes!

It is very difficult for Jamie, as a hearing impaired person, to write a book that relies greatly on the many oral interviews he conducts: "I get someone to transcribe the tapes, often my mother. I double-check anything that is controversial," he said. "Sometimes, people I talk to get a little impatient with me when I have to ask them to repeat what they said. I just say, 'Excuse me, I'm hard of hearing and I need to lip read.' Most are really nice about it, though."

All of his meetings must be done in person, as phone interviews are impractical. Clearly, putting together a book is not easy for Jamie, but he rightly deserves to be called an overcomer.

Besides being a fan of the Wildcats and the Pittsburgh Pirates, Jamie loves to tell about his friendship with one of the greatest baseball players of all time, Roberto Clemente. It started back in the 1960s on a trip to Cincinnati's Crosley Field, where ten-year-old Jamie and his father saw the Reds and Pirates play.

"I was standing in the back of a crowd with my father in a hotel lobby," Jamie explained, "and Roberto Clemente walked through. I had sent him a letter a while before that time. With everybody around him, he looked to the back of the crowd and saw me and told *me* to come to the front. I walked up and passed by the other fans."

What came next will forever stick in Jamie's memory.

"I asked Clemente if he got the letter I sent to him. He didn't know, but he said he'd check. One week later, I received a bunch of stuff in the mail from him. He *did* check," Jamie said proudly. Later, the excited young lad received an autographed bat from the future Hall of Famer, and Vaught later had his name mentioned in several Clemente biographies which were published in the 1970s.

Today, Jamie Vaught is a professor of business administration and accounting at Southeast Kentucky Community and Technical College in Middlesboro, near the Cumberland Gap, where long ago many pioneer settlers entered Kentucky. Being somewhat a pioneer himself, Vaught is a faculty advisor for the school newspaper and writes for several newspapers in Kentucky.

It should be noted that though he lives in a largely silent world, Vaught's brave way of handling his daily challenges provides encouragement to all who seek a full and productive life, regardless of the obstacles.

Mike Howard

'Mountain Santa' Brings Joy and Hope to Neighbors

Mike Howard has some bad memories about some things he did while growing up as one of eleven kids in an eastern Kentucky town. "Guess I was the black sheep of the family," he said.

He recalled one real bad thing he did as a child. "One time I threw a rock from up on the roof and hit my brother in the head," he explained. "I went inside and told my mom I'd killed him."

As it turned out, the injury to his brother wasn't that bad, and it might have been the event that moved his life in a more positive direction.

His neighbors around Wallins Creek, in Harlan County, are very glad to have Mike involved in their lives. Now in his late fifties, Mike is known for his awesome acts of kindness all through the year, and especially during the Christmas season. He proudly wears the nickname "Mountain Santa," and he humbly accepts the praise.

He is truly a good and giving man.

Every year since 1974, Mountain Santa and his helpers have delivered pick-up loads of toys and other treats to both the young and old in the community in the days leading up to December 25. It has grown into a big project. For Christmas 2011, more than one hundred trucks were involved and a hundred and fifty people helped out on the first run.

"The longest run was on Christmas Eve," said Mike. "It's our hometown and it took eleven hours to finish it."

His son, Jordan, was a huge help with the trucking crews that traveled up the mountain sides and into the hollows of Harlan County. Donated toys and treats come from as far away as the city of Louisville and the states of North Carolina, Mississippi, and Tennessee.

Mountain Santa's work of kindness is becoming a big operation, and Mike has a sizeable storage building on his property in Wallins. "We collect donations all during the year," he said. By the time Christmas rolls around, the building is packed with candy, snacks, and of course, the toys. Each treat bag has thirty-two items—packed with the efforts of well over a hundred people.

But Mike reaches out to those in his community in other ways throughout the year. He makes weekly visits to inmates at the local jail, strumming his guitar and singing uplifting songs. He also visits elderly persons at nursing homes around town. There, he is a big hit with residents who look forward to his gifts of milkshakes, bananas and other treats, along with his smile and the attention he gives them. He's often helped neighbors pay their electric bills and likes to call on them to make sure they are safe or need something. Howard also is a good father of two sons and a daughter, and he adores his wife, Barbara.

Mike talks about getting his inspiration to help others from his faith. He says he "heads to the mountain" to get ready for his service. The mountain he talks about is behind his home, which sits along the rippling Wallins Creek on Santa Claus Lane. He likes to go there to pray about doing kind acts for what he calls "old people and widows," along with the children he sees during Christmas season.

"Been doing it for years, sometimes five, six times a week," said Howard. "And if it rains, I take an umbrella. If it snows, I take me a stick." Howard also uses a closet in the family's house as a way to get away and pray. "I just move the shoes in there away," Howard said with a grin.

Mountain Santa is the nickname given him, said Howard, "by some man in Louisville who heard about me." The name is a way to get others interested in being part of the on-going mission. Howard believes that if his heart is right, he'll receive gifts of money from others to help pay for items he buys to give. He often orders his goodies, like candy, fruit and chips he plans to give "not knowing where the money will come from."

But it always does seem to come.

"People will come up to me at the store counter, shake my hand and give me the money," said Howard. He appreciates people like the one who gives twenty dollars a month, but doesn't give their name. A church donates two hundred dollars per month, and there are dozens of people who help with the gift wrapping. And there are the ones who stand outside in the middle of car traffic doing "road block" fundraising.

Tears well up in his eyes when he talks about some of the individuals, those who might be called "Santa's elves," who remember how Mike Howard once helped them get along when times were tough. "They say 'if it weren't for you we never would have had any Christmases. Now we are able to help you,'" he said.

Mike, who is small and lean, doesn't match the hefty body size of Santa Claus, but he has a heart as big as the man from the North Pole. You just have to ask the good folks living in Harlan County who know Mike Howard.

'Bearing Good Tidings to All'
Three Servings of Teddy Bear Love

Dick and Ardi Wilson have shared their cuddly kind of love for over a decade. Taelor Martin went "beary" while she was in kindergarten, and now she is a teenager. Landen Speck, 7, and Briana Stout, 9, are brothers and sisters who have that fuzzy way about them, too.

Following are three stories with a common thread of caring. Each story tells of teddy bear lovers who also like to donate cubbies to others. In so doing, they lift the spirits of people who can *use* their spirits lifted.

Dick and Ardi Wilson

Ardi Wilson remembered how happy she was after finding out on a blind date that her future husband shared something special in common. "I discovered we both liked to collect teddy bears," said Ardi, "and from every date we had from then on, I brought him a teddy bear. I made a little backpack for the bears to put in love notes. Those bears and the notes tell the whole story of the time before we got married."

Even better, the tender moments shared for the Louisville couple were the beginning of a grand story that continues today.

When Dick decided to have a birthday party for Ardi not long before their marriage in November 2000, she suggested he do something out of the ordinary. Ardi requested that Dick ask the party guests to bring a teddy bear for a gift, and that the collected bears be donated to the local branch of Dream Factory. Dream Factory is an organization that helps children who are very ill, and the local chapter was co-founded in Louisville by Dick Wilson.

Dick liked the idea for the party, so on the occasion of Ardi's birthday celebration, the couple accepted 193 bears that helped start an organization of encouragement. Dick and Ardi's personal mission of kindness, called "Ardi's Bears," was born.

Today, the couple figures that their project has resulted in the collection of over thirty-five thousand teddy bears. Besides partnering with the Dream Factory, the loveable and fuzzy comfort toys are donated to other young people in the Louisville area and even, sometimes, outside the area. Often the bears go to needy school children or to those living in orphanages. Five hundred of the bears were given to war-weary Iraqi children by way of American troops. Single mothers at Louisville's Wayside Mission have received bears from the Wilsons, and slightly damaged bears are given to the local Humane Society, where, says Dick, "Dogs love to sleep with them."

Ardi's Bears is an uplifting work of love meant to help those who are hurting. Ardi tends to be the one out in front, the "face" of the project. Dick is the effective, but behind the scenes person. "I see myself as the collaborator," he said.

Money to buy bears is accepted, but donated teddy bears are what Dick and Ardi really like to get. The couple tries to avoid the trappings of a big business with lots of paperwork and paid workers. They seek to keep things simple and effective. "The 'board' (members) is everyone I know because they know I collect bears," said Ardi with a grin.

The couple has set up collection points at local banks, and many friends of the Wilsons take on their own searches for teddy bears to donate. "One person goes to estate sales," said Ardi. "I bet he collected over a thousand bears in the course of two months, and he left them at our back door." Another person collected over two thousand at yard sales. All involved with the bear project do it because it is fun and are inspired to do so by the happily married couple.

Charming little teddy bears, it seems, bring out the best in others—and even grows romances.

Taelor Martin

Kindergartener Taelor Martin heard the talk with her innocent ears. She also watched the TV pictures flashing gloom as Hurricane Katrina reared its ugly head in the Gulf Coast in late summer, 2005.

Just like those with years of perspective, she didn't understand why so many had to suffer, especially other children. All she really knew for sure was that her tender heart wanted to help young kids who are suffering. And so with encouragement from her family and friends, that's just what she did.

Taelor decided that she wanted to collect teddy bears and give them as gifts of kindness to young people. Added to the treat of a teddy bear, Tailor decided she wanted a candy cane tied around the neck of each of the furry stuffed animals. Her parents contacted the St. Joseph Children's Home in their hometown Louisville and found out that Taelor would need forty-two bears in order for every child there to receive one. She had fun making signs to put on collection boxes, and besides telling those in her family, she even got up in front of her church one Sunday and announced her project idea!

The results were amazing, according to Taelor's mother, Stacie Martin: "I honestly thought that we would be lucky to get all forty-two," said Stacie. "However, word spread and she received teddy bears from as far away as California. All in all, she collected somewhere around 230 teddy bears. We then divided them up and took them to several local charities in addition to the orphanage."

In the last few years, Taelor has organized two book drives for charitable causes and is currently working on a drive to help the local animal shelter. Now early in her teen years with a solid background in leading good causes, one can only imagine how she will help change the world for good in the future.

Landen Speck and Briana Stout

Landen Speck and his sister, Briana Stout, understand the joy of receiving a teddy bear as a gift. It's happened to them often and never gets old.

When asked why teddy bears bring them such pleasure, they respond in different ways. "They are so cuddly and they have fur!" says Briana. Landen simply answers with a wide and winning grin, something he does often. Both have a personal collection of bears, and most of the fluffy creatures have names. One is "Beary," another is "Hunter," and one is called "Stripes," to name just a few.

But when the two Winchester children really want to know joy, they turn their hearts outward toward the needs of others, mostly to people they don't even know.

Along with the help of their mother, Daphne Stout, and her husband, Tony, the two have become well-known around Winchester for their teddy bear drive. Their story appeared in the

Winchester Sun, which has made their collecting drive a little easier and is an encouragement to Landen and Briana.

Another thing has helped, too, according to Briana. "My school (Shearer Elementary) lets me talk about it on our news show," said the enthusiastic fourth-grader. They have gathered three hundred of a goal of six hundred bears, both from friends and through drop-off places around town.

The real fun for Landen and Briana, though, is when they deliver the bears at places like the Homeless Coalition and the Fountain Circle, a nursing home, both in Winchester. Their bears have also found new and happy homes at the University of Kentucky Hematology Clinic and to Jarrett's Joycart at the UK Children's Hospital. Their favorite place to share is at the Galilean Home, a Christian mission home and school in Liberty, a place that has taken in children who have been abused, neglected, or abandoned—hundreds of them over many years.

At the Galilean Home, Landen and Briana enjoy meeting people like "George," a kind man who has developmental disabilities. "Landen and I were quiet when we first got there but we saw where people with special needs are really nice," said Briana. The two especially have fun being around the babies in Galilean's "Angel House," where mothers serving prison terms have been taken in for temporary care.

It is clear that Landen and Briana are enjoying the project and plan to keep doing it for a good while. They are well-rounded children with a "we can do" attitude and are unusually wise for their elementary school ages.

Landen's father, Jerod Speck, of Richmond, is amazed by Landen's good nature and spirit. Landen has picked up his father's love of the outdoors, and Jerod shared a memorable time between them: "Once we were hunting late in the evening and we never as much seen a deer. As we packed our stuff, I held my head in frustration. He said in the loudest voice, 'Look how pretty the full moon is, Daddy. We can see the first star from up here.'"

The experience made Jerod stop and think. "At that time, he put me in check. It's not about the hunt. It's about the journey and the little things that seem so bright that us parents take for granted every day," he said.

Landen playfully calls Briana a "tree hugger," and she responds with, "I don't like to kill animals." But even with a few typical sibling differences, their project has brought a special, huggable closeness to the children.

And what is clear is that all who know Landen and Briana are inspired by their innocent zest for life and desire to see others smile a little bit more. Daphne talked about her wishes for the two: "I just want them to be good people. I was taught that we are all made from one God, and I tell them that they're put on this earth to make a difference."

It seems that Landen and Briana understand that lesson well, and they are showing they do by their actions.

Charles Whitaker

'The Can Man' Quietly Helps School Children

Charles Whitaker is a quiet man who lives in the tiny eastern Kentucky town called River, in Johnson County. He's not unfriendly at all, just a little shy. He has soft, gentle eyes that show he is a person who comes in peace and kindness. He is a good, giving, and *forgiving* man. But for the way he has chosen to help children in his community, the locals call him "The Can Man."

In his nineties, Charles gets along very well. Most days, except for Sunday when he goes to church, the white-haired and slender man can be seen around the nearby town of Paintsville, mostly around parking lots. There, he carefully collects aluminum beverage cans to sell at a recycling center in Prestonsburg, in Floyd County. Lots of times, he might be at a neighbor's house with his Ford Ranger pickup truck gathering the cans saved especially for him. On Saturday he'll probably be at the stockyards in Paintsville, where, he said: "I pick up cans all day, even in the winter … four or five bags."

Charles has his own little "recycle-processing" room down in his friend Cort Daniel's basement. There he keeps the cans he smashes with a sledge hammer before he sells them. His project is friendly to the earth and noble, too. He gets paid about 75 cents per pound for his trouble, then he promptly will "just take the money and receipts right over to the school and give it to 'em," he said in his soft and easy way. The place where he delivers the funds is the local Johnson County Christian School, in Paintsville—expecting nothing in return. "Don't even take my gas money out of it," he explained.

Charles has been collecting cans for this purpose since the mid-nineties, and he keeps close account of how much money he has raised (over thirty-six thousand dollars) and how many cans he has gathered and taken to the center. "Two million, working on three million cans. It adds up," he said.

Charles also is driving his third pickup truck since he started doing cans. His first truck simply wore out. A few years ago, Charles was involved in a serious accident with the second truck and spent nineteen days in a local hospital. He got back to collecting cans soon after he was released.

The school Charles supports has about sixty-seven students, grades kindergarten through eight. School board member Jim McKenzie said the money he raises is "often used to help the families who are behind in their payments to the school. It's so good to see people get involved in something like this for no personal reasons other than they just want to help. He does it *sometimes* when he's not feeling well. I've seen him working when he was so weak he should have been in bed."

The Can Man has not been without a bit of adventure, the unwanted kind, while carrying out his project. On one occasion, a sour-mannered man saw Charles crushing cans in a store parking lot and called him names that were hurtful. People who know Charles Whitaker were not surprised at his positive response to the undeserved behavior.

"The man told me that people were saying I was nothing but the belly of a snake who would stoop to do what I was doing," Charles said. "But I forgave him and I don't have any hard feelings." He also said he forgave the bad driver in the wreck that sent him to the hospital. It's the way he lives his faith, and others notice.

He's not one to brag, either. "He's humble, and he's always been that way," said Kym Hitchcock, his great-niece.

Charles simply doesn't see himself as anyone special or any kind of hero. It was almost by accident that he became The Can Man. "There was a lady about ninety-years-old who asked me to start doing the cans for the school," Charles remembered. "She had to quit. It was something (for me) to do. I didn't have anything else to do so I got started doing it. What I do, I do to help the kids."

Quietly, Charles Whitaker goes about the business of helping in a way that most would say is not glamorous or calls attention to him. He sees his efforts as doing something *much* bigger than himself, and the citizens around Johnson County see that, too. They admire and support The Can Man in that work, and all benefit.

Jody Keeley

Using Horses to Help People

The size of Jody Keeley's big heart is matched only by the smile she shares daily with the people around her. She helps individuals with special needs, and she does it in a special way—with the help of gentle, friendly riding horses.

Jody is a special education teacher, but she also gets plenty of care-giving practice at her northern Kentucky home in Verona. That's because her daughter, Hannah, who is in her twenties, needs constant care with severe cerebral palsy. So, Jody works hard teaching people with disabilities and at-risk children for the Kenton County Schools, and she also works hard with Hannah.

But that is not all she does. Lovesome Stables is an after-school program started by her to teach people with disabilities to ride horses. The students range in ages from four to thirty-four.

It's admirable that a person is willing to sacrifice so much of their time and energy to make others' lives better.

"I don't know how she finds the time to do everything she does," said Stephanie Arnold, who has two children in Jody's "horse therapy" program. "Jody is like a beam of sunshine. She always finds a way to take the time (for the kids) that they require and makes each and every one of them feel very special."

There are currently nine carefully chosen horses involved with Lovesome Stables Equitherapy, located at Duane and Paula Gatewood's farm outside Jonesville, a tiny town in Grant County. Jody works with students on Monday nights and Saturday mornings, while Paula Gatewood leads on Wednesday nights. Each has a different way of teaching, but both are good at what they do. Jody has a quiet, easy style, while Gatewood is more outgoing.

It was Paula who kindly offered to host the program at Gatewood Arena. It was a dream of Jody's for ten years, and Duane and Paula have offered important support. Along with the Gatewoods, Jody has many supporters who provide guidance, caring and their skill with horsemanship to make the program work well.

One person travels from Dayton, Ohio to volunteer. Jody's former neighbor, Mark Lehman, started as a Lovesome Stables board member, but he started coming on Saturday mornings. "Got sucked in after I came," he said. Another important team member is Stephanie Sciamanna. She is also a Kenton County educator who has watched Jody devoting her life to students with disabilities for over fifteen years.

According to Jody, the benefits of horseback riding as therapy comes in a natural and enjoyable way.

"The gentle, smooth gait of the horse's movement is similar to the human walk, so it helps with balance, coordination and muscle tone, even with students who are unable to walk on their own," she said. "The horse and rider bond helps the students relax and use self-discipline. It brings about confidence, trust and friendship with this large and warm animal." Jody also explained that a variety of games and exercises are used to help students to learn and communicate.

But it's more than "fun" things that the students gain from therapy.

"We don't just give 'pony rides,'" she said. "Our goal is for each student to become a confident, independent rider. Each week we try to challenge them a little more, but always making sure they can be successful. We annually go to Special Olympics and have 'in home' horse shows two or three times each year for the students to show off their skills for family and friends. They are judged and win medals, trophies, and awards."

Interestingly, the words on the program's logo say: "Where everyone is welcome to horse around."

Linda Gribben has five grandchildren in the program, and she thinks Lovesome is awesome.

"Our grandson, Casey, has many medical problems and had never actually talked to my husband and I," she said. "After riding an hour in the class, he was helped off the horse and he headed directly to Terry and I with a big smile on his face and he high-fived both of us. As he was leaving that day, he yelled 'I love you, Grandma and Grandpa!' I call it a miracle. Jody helps make those miracles happen over and over."

Lovesome Stables has about fifty participants, but Jody dreams of something even greater. "I'd like to someday have a working farm that's run by adults with disabilities. It would have an art studio and the horseback riding program," she said.

But even though Jody's program has not yet reached the level she'd like, it requires a huge effort by her to keep the current program so successful. In her personal life, she has great responsibility at home with the needs of her daughter. Her position as a teacher requires much time and energy. And finally, the Lovesome Stables program is almost a full-time job—even with the wonderful help she receives.

For that, Mark Lehman praised Jody's dedication.

"She gets emails and texts at 11:30 at night. She raises money for this program, and she has horse shows with awards and medals for the kids, and she's involved in the Special Olympics," he said. "For eighteen years, since I met her, Jody has been my hero."

Jody doesn't like to brag about her part in the success of Lovesome Stables. "Lovesome has been a real exercise in faith for me and I look forward to the journeys ahead. We like to think of Lovesome as an oasis from the world, a positive place where we are all valued and accepted the way we are," she said.

Her friend Stephanie Sciamanna noted Jody's outstanding personal qualities. "Jody has patience and perseverance. She makes sure things get done. Until that product is done, she's going to stick to it."

Lovesome Stables brings joy and high hopes for all involved. Jody offered the example of her teenage son's change of heart when he participated.

"One day, I dragged him down there and he grumbled the whole way. When he got there, he commented that this place was just *too* positive. It was impossible to stay mad here," she said. "We often say the therapy is not just for the students. Our volunteers get as much or more out of working here as the students do. It helps you put everything in perspective."

And for those who watch Jody Keeley in action, they see a truly admirable person—one who is dedicated to helping others saddle up and ride high.

Tim Farmer

Outdoorsman Inspires after Losing
Use of Right Arm

Tim Farmer had an exciting future planned. The 20-year-old was having a rockin' good time in Marine Corps basic training camp back in 1984. He looked forward to making the Marines a career, though he also played with the idea of being a professional musician. Things looked bright for Tim. He had lots of energy and was ready to be a grand success. And whatever his future would look like, he especially knew that it would include his love of the outdoors, with plenty of fishing and hunting. He had been doing that all his young life, and it was very important to him.

But while returning to the Marine boot camp after a visit to his parents in eastern Kentucky, Tim was involved in a motorcycle accident. It nearly took his life. He spent about a year in hospitals in West Virginia, Maryland and Walter Reed Military Hospital in Washington, D.C. Though he survived the motorcycle crash, he now had to deal with a huge, new challenge. He lost the use of his right arm.

It took Tim a while before he understood fully how his life would change. On an occasion while taking a cafeteria meal in

Walter Reed Hospital, Tim tried to carry his well-stocked tray with only his "good" left arm. The items on the tray fell with a loud noise, causing a moment of embarrassment as on-lookers stared at him and became silent. Tim was shook up badly, but it helped him realize something very important. "I knew then that everything was going to be different in my life, that I was going to have to understand that and make the best of it," explained Tim. "I was a one-armed guy."

As soon as he was released from the hospital and honorably discharged from the Marine Corps, he went back to Grayson, his home. Tim had missed his outdoors time with hunting and fishing while he was receiving treatment. Determined, the young man with a severe disability began to try different ways to do his favorite hobby. His positive mental outlook would not allow him to give up. "The brain is set up to have you use both hands in most of your activities," explained Tim, "so you have to train it to allow you to do things with just one hand. There is usually a way. You just have to figure out what it is."

So with time and lots of practice, Tim learned to cast his fly fishing line out and then use his mouth to draw the line back, or use a spin-casting reel by cranking the handle with his mouth. A belt around his waist held a tube in front that could hold his rod securely, freeing his left hand for use. He also figured out how to rest a rifle on his left shoulder, aim and shoot targets or game accurately. His dream of getting back into the fun of the woods and water by making a few personal adaptations, or changes, was now being realized!

As Tim began to feel comfortable using his new, adaptive skills, he also needed a job. He briefly attended college part-time, and he took several temporary jobs after he was married. He wanted a career, however, that he could love. After a few short years, he found just what he wanted. And it was like getting paid to do his favorite hobby.

Tim moved his wife and two young girls to Frankfort in 1989 to work for the Kentucky Fish and Wildlife Department as a fisheries technician. "I was in 'high cotton.' I had a uniform and a name tag and everything," said Tim, in remembering the huge step he took in employment while overcoming his disability. Tim was happy to be paid for doing what was like a hobby for him, and his technician job continued for several years. But then another break came his way. For Tim Farmer, the "high cotton" grew even taller.

That break happened in 1994 when the popular television program, *Kentucky Afield,* was looking for a new host. They soon found the ideal person ... a young fisheries technician inside the Kentucky Department of Fish and Wildlife by the name of Tim Farmer. Besides being dynamic and enthusiastic, the new host presented an amazing example of a person who stared down a serious disability and showed what is possible with hard determination. Tim quickly became popular across the state in his new position. Along with good people working alongside him, the program has won two Emmy awards in recent years.

Tim remembers the important lessons he learned as a young boy while hunting game in Kentucky's woods and fishing its waters. He wants to share what he learned with young people today as he gets the opportunity. He often includes kids in episodes of Kentucky Afield, and he makes a point to meet and encourage them as they participate in department events.

Some of Tim's most memorable times have come while sharing with children with disabilities. He shows them how he uses his special adaptations to live an active life. His message to those watching him is useful and quite simple: "It shouldn't be a big issue," says Tim. "Rather than handicap or disability, I prefer to call it an aggravation."

The way Tim Farmer handles his "aggravations" every day gives others a good example to follow. He enjoys his life, but it is not always easy. He is never free from some pain in his shoulder area of his injured arm, and his "good" arm often aches because he uses it so much. Still he smiles and seldom complains. Others are lifted in spirit. They, in turn, are good examples to others. You get the picture.

Tim has always believed "things happen for a reason." By being an inspiration to others through overcoming a serious physical challenge he acquired when he was 20, Tim has found his reason. And truly, the rest of us are better off for it.

Judy Hensley

Bringing Her Classroom to Life

When Ms. Judy Hensley starts talking classroom projects, she doesn't need to suggest topics. Her students come up with the ideas themselves. Then, she just stands back and watches the students' excitement spill over. It often spills over into their local community—and sometimes even farther.

Judy has faith in her pupils at Wallins Middle/Elementary School in eastern Kentucky, enough to move mountains, or, rather, to keep mountains *from being moved*. To explain, it's been over a decade ago that her class of seventh and eighth-graders in the Harlan County school got fired up about nearby Black Mountain, the tallest in Kentucky. The top of the mountain was scheduled to be "scalped" by what is called mountain-top removal (MTR). With MTR, coal companies blow off the top of a mountain with explosives, then gather the coal.

Though there are people in Appalachia who are for MTR, Judy's class took a stand against it, at least in regard to Black Mountain. The students first heard about the news from a classmate. "A little girl who was very shy had me read her letter to the class," she said, "and the words basically said: 'Don't blow it up!' It made the other kids wonder why the coal company didn't want to save the highest mountain in the state."

Students were excited and wanted to do something to "save" the well-known mountain. Their teacher gave them the freedom to do the project. Judy is skilled in watching projects grow from the interests of the students because she's trained in the noted Foxfire Method of teaching. Using the Foxfire Method, she coaches but relies mainly on decisions made by students—having *them* decide what and how they will study and present their topic. Her answer to the question, "What will your class do this year?" usually gets a simple answer from Judy: "Whatever they come up with … I'm not really sure yet."

The Black Mountain project became one of the most exciting in her teaching career. "The class started doing research and then traveled on buses to deliver letters to the Office of Surface

Mining," said Judy. "It was a field trip to practice freedom of speech."

People around the community were showing signs of concern about what was happening with Black Mountain. "There were others already meeting and talking about it, but it had not made it into the media," said Judy. "When the students delivered those letters, a newspaper reporter covered it. The Associated Press picked it up. Then bam, bam, bam. The story made it to Ted Koppel's Nightline and even was featured in a book called Hope & Heroes."

After her class delivered the letters, they teamed with students from Rosenwald Dunbar Elementary School, in Jessamine County, to travel to Frankfort, the state capital, to speak to a legislative committee. "That school, with teachers Sandy Adams and Barb Greenleaf, got the ball rolling in central Kentucky," she said.

No doubt with some credit going to Judy's class, hearings were held concerning the Black Mountain MTR issue, and it was resolved the way her class wished.

"It came to a good resolution, so about twenty-thousand acres at the top of Black Mountain were preserved," Judy said. "There were endangered species there such as Indiana bats, salamanders and indigenous plants. Black Mountain wasn't only significant because it was the state's highest mountain, but also because there were indigenous plants and animals not found anywhere else."

During classroom lessons, she made sure that the students understood the need to listen to different sides of discussions. People who worked in the mining industry were invited to present their perspective on mountain-top removal. Interestingly, one class member was a grandson of a mining engineer.

The project that was started by Judy's class ended with a memorable event. The Wallins and Dunbar students held hands around the base of Black Mountain in a huge ceremony of celebration and unity!

Another of her classes helped in protection of eastern Kentucky's Blanton Forest, the largest "old growth" woods in Kentucky. A noted quilter worked with one of Judy's classes to craft "angel quilts." Her students have often made pen pal relationships an important part of their learning activities, and another of her classes worked with some Berea College students in an "Aging in Appalachia" project. Together, they talked to senior citizens in Harlan County and made a DVD of the experience.

Her sixth-grade classes have published an on-going book series called *Mountain Mysteries.* Judy is a published writer, also. She writes short stories and has authored two elementary level books, *Terrible Tina* and *Sir Thomas the Eggslayer.* She dreams of becoming a full-time writer in the future.

Besides teaching at Wallins Creek, she previously was a part-time instructor at Southeast Community College. She often sings solos at her church and is a talented photographer.

Her greatest joy comes when she helps a young person grow to be their best self. She works extra hard and won't easily give up on students who are acting difficult or causing trouble. She puts it this way: "It's sometimes difficult to uncover the jewel inside a child, but kids are so much worth the effort. They're just full of surprises."

Judy has an interesting way of explaining the importance of a teacher.

"Teaching is one of those rare careers where you get to be an artist, a singer, a philosopher and a psychologist," said Judy, who has an open and friendly style that helps create a good student-teacher relationship. "Every person deserves a positive stroke each day and I do just the best I can."

Judy Hensley is the kind of teacher each of us always wanted to have in our own classroom. She's one who has a quiet but confident manner; she prefers to listen rather than do all the talking. Being fair and serving a larger purpose are guiding principles she lives every day. By doing so, she inspires others to do likewise.

Dr. George Wright

'No Excuses' Attitude Leads to Huge Success

When George Wright was growing up in poverty in Lexington over fifty years ago, he felt like he was living in shame and didn't want others to know about it. It got worse when his parents divorced. His grades were bad, even though he had a good mind.

"I always acted real out-going and was a show-off," said George. "I didn't let people know of the hurt in my life."

He received no sympathy from his mother, however. She didn't want him to feel sorry for himself and quit doing his responsibilities. "My mother taught me there were 'no excuses for not doing well in school,'" said George. She also made it clear he *would* go to college someday. "And she told me that if I went around with a chip on my shoulder, people weren't going to help me."

It took years before Wright fully accepted his mother's advice. Eventually, her words helped motivate him to succeed in a huge way. He achieved highly in college and became a professor and administrator at that level, and is now the president of a university. Now, well-educated and with years of hard-earned wisdom, Dr. George Wright gives much of the same advice he heard from his mother to students at his university.

But back to George's early years. He remembered feeling relief when his mother and father moved the family to a much nicer neighborhood, but that changed again when his parents started having trouble and got a divorce. "My father's drinking began to get worse, causing our family problems," he said, "so when my parents divorced, we had financial problems and had to move back to Charlotte Court."

George's sense of shame and the feeling of being "not as good as others" became worse. His poor grades and bad behavior continued. Then, after attending the integrated Leestown Middle School, George moved on to the mostly white Lexington Lafayette High School in 1966, where his older sister was enrolled. The three years he spent there were interesting, if not highly successful.

"I was usually the only black in my classes there," he said. "In history class, I'd participate in the discussions and people saw me as 'the history person.'" But that was the good part. "I didn't turn in many of my assignments or projects," he said. "I didn't see good enough reasons for doing the work, so I didn't. Somebody has to show me good reason to do things, or I won't do them."

George graduated from Lafayette High School in 1968 with a poor 1.89 grade point average. It showed his poor study habits rather than his high ability. But during that senior year, something happened to him that began to change his way of looking at things. He had just gotten off work one night from his part-time job at Lexington's Idle Hour Country Club. "When the city bus came to take me to Charlotte Court, I saw some friends on it," George explained. "I did not get on the bus because I didn't want them to see where I was going. I ended up walking a long way home in the cold."

The experience changed young George's attitude. "I cried and I cussed," he said. "When I got home, I was done with feeling sorry for myself. I decided then that something had to be done."

Surviving high school, he enrolled at the University of Kentucky, a place where "people would encourage me in all sorts of ways," he remembered. His grades improved a lot, and as he started working toward two degrees in the subject of history, two special people noticed him and they made a positive difference for George.

One person would be his future wife, Valerie Ellison. They dated for a while, but George "finally got serious with ... when I noticed her holding hands with a track star." The two were married while at UK, and she was a great encouragement to the "new" George Wright. Valerie Wright is now an associate editor for *Texas Monthly* magazine. They have been married over forty years, a union that brought them two children.

Another person who made a difference while George was in college was T. Harry Williams, a well-known historian. Williams was impressed with George's work in one of his classes, so he wrote a letter to Duke University, one of the most respected schools in the United States. George was accepted there and received a three-year scholarship and four hundred dollars a month for living expenses. He received his Ph.D in history there, and was the first American black at Duke to do so.

The Wrights then returned to Lexington. This time, George came as an assistant professor at his beloved UK. His style as a teacher was strong and he liked to challenge young people's thinking.

In 1980, the Wright family moved to the University of Texas at Austin where he was a very popular professor. He predicted to a class there that he "would be a college president some day." By the year 1993, he was back at Duke University with several important positions in administration. From there, George became the number two person in the administration at the University of Texas at Arlington, serving for eight years. This latest position was the final tune-up for a huge job … one that made his pre–diction several years before come true.

In 2003, Dr. George Wright, who had struggled with his grades while growing up poor in Lexington's inner-city many years before, became the seventh president of Prairie View A&M

University, near Houston, Texas. He received the opportunity to speak at UK's graduation ceremonies in 2004, a bit of "icing on the cake" back in his hometown. He also has published three books and is working on another about African-American history.

With the positive way things have turned out in his life, George feels like a blessed man. "It's never been far from my mind living in Charlotte Court and walking home that night in the cold," he said. "I don't know why I had to live like that and I don't know why I live like this now."

George can "live like this now" because of the new focus he put on giving his best effort in his schoolwork when he set foot on the UK campus back in 1968. He wishes he had started earlier, but he understands that is all behind him now, and he learned from those experiences.

His wife watched the change in him as her husband gained success as he matured. "He really buys into the idea that he is willing to work harder and longer than anyone else. He's up at 5:30 a.m. Monday through Friday," said Valerie. "He tells his students that education made all the difference in his life, that it will do the same for them and, by extension, the members of their families."

George admitted: "I'm not that smart. I work hard ... and I make no excuses for anything."

Just like his mother told him.

Grace Harvey

Finding Joy through Giving

A West Jessamine Middle School student in Nicholasville is finding that true joy does not come from having things, but by being a "giver of things." Grace Harvey, a petite and energetic honor student, makes it a practice to act out her religious faith through her compassionate efforts for others. She also gives some of her hard-earned money to help less fortunate people. And, in an awesome display of grace—like her first name shows—she once gave up a new bicycle she had won in a school contest to allow another student to get the prize!

"Grace is such a wonderful student," said Heidi Crabtree, who was her fifth grade teacher. "She has such a generous, kind heart toward all her classmates and friends."

The evidence for Crabtree's statement is strong, to be sure.

Grace worked with enthusiasm during Christmas, 2011, to support an organization called Food for the Hungry. She raised money for some very practical uses. "I bought de-worming medicine for five hundred kids, some Tippy Taps (a basic hand washing station), a year's worth of water purification tablets for a family, and a pair of chickens," said Grace.

During the same period, she worked through her place of worship, the Southland Christian Church in Jessamine County, to help with the church's goal of packing 1.1 million meals to send to the poor country of Haiti.

There are regular activities in which Grace volunteers in order to be a "giver" to others, too.

"On the third Saturday of every month," Grace explained, "I go to my grandma's church and they do something called a 'manna-meal,' where people come who don't have a lot of money or anything like that and they come and have lunch." The church cooks the food and provides drinks and desserts. Volunteers also serve by waiting on tables. "It's a lot of fun and you learn that you don't have it as tough or hard as some people do," she remarked. Grace finds time, too, to help every Saturday night in Southland's church nursery with very young children.

While a student at Brookside Elementary, Grace used her knack for being lucky to put a big smile on the face of another student at the school. In contest drawings the school had for perfect attendance achievers, she won a bicycle in the third grade and twice in the fifth grade. After winning the second time in the fifth grade, she shocked the school staff and students in an uplifting, unusual way. "I told them to draw again because I already had two bikes at home," Grace said. "It just gives me joy when I help other people."

Grace's parents, Scott and Greta Harvey, admire what their oldest child has done for others.

"We are so proud of her loving and giving heart," Greta said. "We pray all the time that we (the family) will all see others as Jesus does and love them as He does. Grace has always been generous and kind toward others, and especially those who have been overlooked."

Young Grace Harvey has learned early the importance of living unselfishly for the benefit of others. She is a fine example for her peers and a wonderful instrument of love—and she likely is just getting started on this positive path.

Brian Huybers

Youth Uses Eagle Scout Project for Flight 5191 Memorial

Many people say bad things about young people in America today. They say that our youth are lazy and they don't appreciate the truly important things in life—like doing for others and being unselfish. Some even say that our country's future is doomed to failure because the young generation seems to care only about themselves.

Well, not so fast.

Meet teenager Brian Huybers. He doesn't fit the unkind words spoken about his age group. In fact, the folks around Richmond, in Madison County, know what good this young man has done. They can take you to Lake Reba Recreational Park and show you the beautiful memorial fountain built to honor six persons from Madison County. They were among the victims of the tragic August 27, 2006, Flight 5191 airline crash at Bluegrass Airport, in Lexington, which claimed forty-nine lives. Folks can tell you that Brian played a huge role in making the memorial, and he did that by helping design it and spending much of his time and energy to raise the needed money for the project.

Brian got started in September 2007, thirteen months after the air crash, when he was sixteen. The Boy Scout began searching for a project that would reward him the Eagle Scout Badge, a great honor. He wanted the special project to be something he really *wanted* to do, something to focus both his heart and mind. He knew it would be difficult, but he also knew it would be worthwhile. It took some time for him to decide.

"First, I was just going through possible projects like putting shingles on or winterizing cabins at a church camp, plus a few other things," Brian said. Those ideas didn't catch fire with the high school junior at Madison Central High. But then his troop's assistant scoutmaster, Whitney Dunlap, came to him with an idea: Why not create some kind of memorial to those from the community who died in Flight 5191? That suggestion hit home with Brian. He remembered watching TV and seeing blue buses carrying family members of the victims to the scene of the horrible accident.

The idea for the memorial became his choice for earning the Eagle Scout, and he enthusiastically got started on the project.

The memorial planned would be a wonderful sight. The eight-thousand pound granite fountain showed forty-nine doves—the total number of crash victims. The doves were nicely carved into the stone and flew in different directions. Sparkling water would flow over the doves. Brian promised to help raise the twenty-seven thousand dollars cost for the memorial.

Brian knew that fundraising requires speaking to lots of people in groups. That was difficult because he tended to be shy in those situations. "Asking people for money was the least favorite thing Brian did, but he got better as he started doing it," said Michele Huybers, his mother. Brian mailed letters asking for money and also wrote notes for the talks he would give to community groups. Michele served as Brian's "editor."

Soon, he started on his "speaking tour" at places like his church and the local Kiwanis Club. He appeared in his Boy Scout outfit, wearing his brownish hair in a long ponytail. He was a bit nervous. He received guidance along the way from his friends and felt their encouragement. His goal was to gain the rank of Eagle Scout, but even more, to provide a kind and lasting tribute to his Madison County community.

His efforts paid off. Positive news returned his way from the letters sent. His audiences where he spoke responded well. After several months, the teenager raised nearly seven thousand dollars, and the city government promised to pay the rest.

The memorial was dedicated at the Lake Reba site on August 24, 2008. It was a day that Brian would never forget. During the special ceremony, Boy Scouts released six white doves, representing the local crash victims. Someone played a bagpipe. Each person present felt a warm heart. Brian Huybers stood tall that day, knowing that he was an important reason for what was happening at the event.

Brian was careful to give due credit to others, too. "I could never have done it without my family's help," said Brian. "They were with me from the start." He also mentioned others, including family members of the victims as important in helping the Flight 5191 Memorial become a reality.

Brian's father, Lawrence Huybers, said that at first his son was not sure the memorial idea would be approved as an Eagle Scout project because it would be so difficult to do. "But I think Brian would have continued on it even if it were not," said the proud father. "Brian had gotten so involved in it and wanted it to be completed."

And what are the most important things Brian learned from his experience with the memorial?

"I learned not to be shy and that you've got to do certain stuff with a lot of organizations to make money, and you always have to be talking to different people," he said, "I was actually surprised by myself."

Mr. Dunlap's duties as a scoutmaster have allowed him to get to know Brian well. He bragged on his scout, saying that Brian had "really stepped up his life" since he gained leadership experience with the memorial project.

"Brian has been a 'sleeper,'" he said, "and for a long time was more interested in his garage band than campouts. But when he got with the Eagle Scout project, he really started to run with it."

He saw Brian go from one not interested to become the senior patrol leader of his troop. "On a recent Scout trail hike, Brian volunteered to stay back with another boy who was suffering from heat exhaustion," he said. "He was the most mature Scout we had and he showed a lot of leadership."

Brian now is enrolled at Eastern Kentucky University, Richmond, and is taking on the challenges of being a music major. Don't bet against him succeeding.

Brian is showing the world that there are some really fine young people around today who are good and unselfish role models. Just go visit the Flight 5191 Memorial and see for yourself.

Mary Lou Boal

*Local Travel Guide Brings Comfort
to Those across the World*

It seems like Mary Lou Boal never sits still. She works at a job where she is always traveling and finding good travel experiences for others. Being around her is a positive experience. Her words are uplifting and she has an easy laugh that puts people at ease.

Mary Lou is a compassionate lady who gets things done for those in need. She reaches out to her community, her state and also in another place, she says, that is "forgotten by the world."

Madisonville is her long-time home, but it's really only a nice "parking place" for Mary Lou, who is now in her early seventies. She helps her customers find enjoyable travel experiences through her Total Travel Service agency and has personally taken people on tours to seventy-five countries since starting her business in 1982.

A country called Cambodia in distant Asia has especially captured Mary Lou Boal's imagination and ignited a fire inside her to be a friend to a few of the fourteen million people there. She has worked heroically to bring aid and comfort to the people of this war-torn, poor nation that had many of its citizens killed or maimed by the horrible Khymer Rouge government leaders of the 1970s, who planted millions of explosive land mines. Reports are that one in three-hundred and fifty of Cambodia's citizens have suffered the loss of a leg or arm. It's a problem that still lingers today, about forty years after the inhumane landmines were set in the ground.

Mary Lou played an important role in placing over a thousand wheelchairs in Cambodia to support those suffering from the explosions. She has also supported a children's hospital there. Both projects most clearly define what means most to her. Working through an organization called Free Wheelchairs Mission *(freewheelchairsmission.org),* Mary Lou spoke to anyone who would listen to her sad story of the Cambodian people's misfortune.

She got her business involved, too. Her message to listeners was that the Cambodians are "gentle, polite, and hard-working people who aren't ones looking for a hand-out, but a hand-up." She explained further: "While there, I even came across what is known as a 'butterfly restaurant', where children are paid to collect and release butterflies for money needed at school," she said. That impressed her.

The important action of raising money and shipping the wheelchairs to Cambodia was not all that she did. She also traveled to the country with her friend, Laura Teague, to make sure that the chairs arrived at the correct destination and were received by the intended individuals.

The two Kentuckians traveled to a place in rural Cambodia where the chairs were to be distributed. There, they enjoyed a feast of joy. "It was from no legs to mobility," Mary Lou said. "Each wheelchair was designated for a particular person, and as they received them, they were soon up and running and happy. It took so many people to see that these people got their chairs, and my excitement was seeing it through."

Laura remembers how they sat through an hour of speech-making by officials, then watched as the recipients crawled toward their chairs—moving forward using wooden blocks on their hands. "Many had no legs, one leg, or a leg that didn't work," Teague said. "It was an amazing sight to watch."

Mary Lou first found out about the medical needs of the Cambodians through being shown the Angkor Hospital for Children in Siem Reap. The hospital didn't have enough equipment and only fifty beds. Her heart was touched, and when she returned to her home in Madisonville, she put her business staff to work helping collect items for the hospital to use. "We've got to help, girls," she said to the employees.

Madisonville citizens answered their requests, and soon the hospital received important supplies and money. Today, she encourages others to continue the effort by working through an organization called Friends Without a Border.

The always alert woman has compassion for those in the United States who have experienced catastrophes. In the spring of 1999, Mary Lou led a group called "Helping Hands of Hopkins County, Kentucky," to answer the call of need in the tornado-ravaged area of Oklahoma. When Hurricane Katrina did its terrible damage in 2005, again she led a community effort to fill a tractor-trailer truck with supplies. She found a volunteer driver, along with making sure a waiting group was there to receive the goods.

Mary Lou is good at watching out for the details in the projects. "I am a good organizer," she said, "but the Madisonville community has been tremendous in supporting the projects."

The Rev. Don McLaughlin, Mary Lou's minister at the Madisonville First Christian Church, described her as "one who has a wonderful heart for mission to help people in need" and "she uses creative ways to find resources and is persistent. Mary Lou's enthusiasm is contagious. She has a natural personality for helping and her motivation comes from her faith." Her friend Laura Teague described Mary Lou as "dedicated, energetic, and compassionate … an 'Energizer Bunny' who I could not keep up with when we were in Cambodia."

Mary Lou's good-hearted ways likely stem from the way she was lovingly taken in as a baby by her father's sister after her mother died. "I was treated as well as everyone else in the family, with plenty of caring," she said. She has fond memories of international missionaries, many who were not Americans, having Sunday dinner in her home. "I saw the good treatment and respect shown them, and I can still see the image in my mind today."

Tom Clinton, the former editor of Madisonville's local newspaper, said that she "always seems to look on the bright side and she has the energy of a person half her age."

One might call Mary Lou Boal the "ambassador of caring to the world," and that name would be well-earned.

Kendall Harvey

Three-Wheel Offering

When Kendall Harvey retired as a building contractor a few years ago, he didn't really have a plan to keep him busy. He wasn't one who liked to fish or hunt, and he didn't particularly like watching TV. He wasn't even much of a Kentucky Wildcat basketball fan.

Kendall began to wonder if he did the right thing by quitting a job he did so well, and he soon got a little bored. So, even though he had some health problems, he thought about returning to his building career.

But one day he met a child with Down syndrome at a local restaurant in his town, Columbia, in Adair County. That meeting turned Kendall in a different and rewarding direction. "I looked at the boy and asked him if he had a bike," said Kendall, "and he said 'Yes, it was tore up and it was getting fixed.'"

The boy's mother looked at Kendall with knowing eyes. "He can't ride one," she said. "He just *told* you that."

"Well, he's getting ready to ride one," said Kendall, eyes twinkling. After finding out a little more information about the child, the kind-hearted man went home and began to build a three-wheel bike. Within a week, the young boy was presented, sized up and made to meet his needs—a sharp new three wheeler.

Kendall saw how happy the boy was, and that was all he needed to begin a new, and happier, retirement. He has now made over one-hundred-fifty of the three-wheel bikes for those with special needs, mostly children.

Kendall doesn't charge for his services. He simply likes to help people. He's been at his good work for about a decade in his downstairs workshop at his home in Columbia. He has a nice little system going. He receives donated bikes from places like local stores, then takes them apart and combines with other bike parts to make his own special brand. Other businesses give him scrap wood, metal and even pieces of carpet to use to make the three wheelers look good.

Kendall is a content man while putting the bikes together. "He sometimes stays down there a long time," said his wife, Cecile. "He cares for everybody and the Lord has given him the ability to do these things to help others."

Kendall has a picture album of the recipients with their bikes. A big smile comes over his face as he describes each person. "I built this little girl one and put dolls on it. She outgrew them, then I put a radio on it," he said. Pointing to another picture, he explained the boy's dreams. "This little fellow looks like he is about three, but he's really eleven. He wants to be a lawyer and he's sharp as a tack." And there are more. "See this one. She runs up and hugs me every time she sees me. One of the little boys, when he got his bike, said 'Am I dreaming?' It made my day," Kendall said.

Rod and Carole Embry, of Bowling Green, were happy to see their Down's syndrome son, Alex, receive a red three wheeler from Harvey. "Because of his selflessness, generosity, and genuine care for others, Mr. Harvey is a hero in our eyes," said Rod.

The Adair County community knows Kendall as one with a caring heart, but they also know of him as a person who likes a little adventure. Several years ago, Harvey built his own "paraplane." The odd-looking flying machine looks like a three wheeler with a parachute attached. He was inspired by the fun he had in his earlier days with hang gliding.

"One Fourth of July, I flew that thing right onto the front yard of the Columbia courthouse," he said. When his wife was asked if she flew up there with him, she laughed and said, "No, somebody had to stay on the ground and pray." His three wheeler flying days, said Kendall, "are probably over."

Kendall and Cecile are a couple with strong religious faith, and their youngest son ministers to a large church in the South. While Cecile teaches and Kendall "hands out bulletins" in their local Nazarene church that Kendall built forty years ago, it is clear Kendall shows his faith most powerfully through his three-wheeler work. And, as long as he stays healthy, it appears he will continue. "I started and couldn't get stopped," he said, matter-of-factly.

And that's a good thing, because there are many Kentuckians blessed by Kendall Harvey's three-wheel offering.

Note: *Because of recent health problems, Kendall Harvey has had to discontinue his three-wheel bike project, but he still feels joyful seeing the many lives that have been made happier because of his unselfish desire to use his special talent for others.*

Fanestia Massey

Uplifting to Others after a Terrible Loss

It's difficult to think of a more painful experience than the loss of a child. It is likely that no one can truly understand the deep hurt unless it is *their* child who died. Fanestia Massey does understand because her youngest son, Preston, was killed in an auto accident a few years ago.

There is a big hole in the heart and a feeling that never entirely goes away, even as time passes. Just ask Fanestia and her husband, Roy. But even with the daily burden she carries, Fanestia has found ways to use the experience with her son to help uplift others.

"Project Graduation Night" at Caldwell County High School in the western Kentucky town of Princeton, on May 22, 2004, was a special time when graduating seniors came together to celebrate and have a good time—safely and without the dangers involved with alcohol abuse. All thought this night would be joyful and safe for the sons and daughters of the parents who organized the program.

Preston's nice smile, energy, and pleasing personality were well-known to those around the community of Princeton. He was popular, was a member of the high school baseball team and active in his church. He also liked to share his music. "He took his guitar, named 'Grace,' everywhere," said Fanestia, "and his many friends loved to hear it be played."

Fanestia recalled the events of that night at the high school. "There was a large turnout of kids because we did fun things like Jello wrestling and we gave kids the chance to play games and win money and stay there all night," she said. "When it was over, Preston talked about how he had had the 'best time of his life.'"

But about 6:30 the next morning, the sleepy Preston Massey decided to drive home while his parents stayed at the school and cleaned up after the event. About fifteen minutes after Preston drove away, Fanestia and Roy also left, not knowing that their happy mood would soon change to shock and sadness.

"The accident happened less than a mile from home," Fanestia remembered. "My first words when I saw it were 'Oh, my, it's Preston.' Before Roy got our vehicle stopped, I jumped out. It was bad. They weren't supposed to but they let me ride in the ambulance. I did not want to leave my child."

At the hospital, the sad words—that Preston had died—were gently spoken to Fanestia and Roy. Along with the crushing news, there was a question asked them. Would the couple, while there was still time, allow doctors to take living organs from their son's body in order to help others?

In those dark moments, Fanestia thought of Preston's kind and helping spirit. He had planned to become a nurse after being a comforting caregiver for his dying grandfather.

"Being a donor was Preston's last chance to help others," Fanestia said. Permission was given, and Preston's corneas in each eye were transplanted within forty-eight hours. Today, a living part of the special young man is providing a better life of sight for two persons, one living in Kentucky and the other in Indiana. Also, Preston's donated orthopedic tissues helped create seventy-five bone grafts to use for doing surgery, and sixty-two patients have benefited. Preston's compassionate nature is shown even in his death.

Fanestia talks to anyone who will listen about donating organs, and she works hard to continue Project Graduation. She also started "Preston Massey's Project Pick Me Up" to encourage students at the graduation event to have drivers take them home. She likes to gently explain to the students that "Preston would tell you not to drive home … "

Fanestia and her faithful parent group do the work of raising money for the project. Wendy Fuller of Dawson Springs said that Fanestia "has been a rock for many families that have lost their children." Best friend Teresa Cash talked of Massey's kind and easy way of encouraging others to pledge to donate their organs by having it stated on their driver's license. "Fanestia never pushes anyone about it. She just uses any opportunity she has to let others know," Teresa said. "Her most admirable quality is that she has the ability to relate to any age group."

Fanestia works in the Caldwell County High School office where she has a chance to share and be a friendly face to people every day. She doesn't shy away from telling visitors about the good-looking guy on her computer screensaver, Preston—and his story. She is uplifting to parents concerned about the behavior of their children. She encourages them to appreciate the positive things and not to fight big battles over little things.

Fanestia Massey knows that the sting of Preston's loss will always be with her, but hopes that a larger miracle will be worked as the lives of others are improved through her life of service. Melissa Earnest, an educator and friend, spoke of Fanestia's positive influence: "There is definitely no telling how far she has reached out and touched people, even beyond the borders of our small town and our county. When you throw a stone into a pool of water, the ripples continue on and on and I believe that's what Fanestia has been—a solid rock that has rippled the waters of our lives."

NOTE: For information regarding"Preston Massey's Pick Me Up," contact Fanestia Massey at email fanestia@mchsi.com. *Information about tissue and organ donation can be found at* http://trustforlife.org.

Russell Vassallo
Friend of Animals

It was in the year 2000, and Russell Vassallo was down in the dumps, like he had been most of his life.

It was no wonder. The New Jersey native lived a tough life. When he was a baby, a bad ear infection almost killed him, and it hurt his ability to hear. He had bronchial pneumonia, probably caused by allergies. Young Russell spent a lot of time by himself in his bedroom because of his illnesses. To make matters worse, the kids in his neighborhood in Newark made fun of him being short. He often felt rejected and unloved.

But thankfully, some hope came his way in the middle of those childhood struggles. It was in the form of a small, Pomeranian dog called Palsy. The two had wonderful times together playing outside in the yard for about an hour a day. Palsy, like his name hinted, was a true "pal" to Russell. Their fun time was a memory he never forgot—and many years later it helped him change his life for the better.

When Russell was growing into full adulthood and while moving away from his neighborhood, there were many more problems nagging him. He was thrown out of two high schools. Later, he experienced serious problems in his first marriage, both with his wife and also their children. He was thrown from a horse and suffered a broken hip and ribs. He battled colon cancer and, as a lawyer, once nearly got into a fistfight during a courtroom trial. "I always thought of myself as strong-willed, and I had a lot of anger inside me," he said of his bad temper.

But Russell Vassallo's story doesn't end with all those bad things. He remarried, left New Jersey and bought a 224-acre farm in Casey County in the 1990s. There, he decided to raise and help distressed animals. He wanted to change; he was tired of relying on medicine to help him from being sad. So Russell decided to boost himself by opening up to what he called his "animal friends," remembering how important Palsy was to him so many years ago. And, with the help of wife Virginia, he began a new career as an author. Animals became his main topic.

His first book, titled *Tears and Tales: Stories of Animal and Human Rescue,* shows a lot about who Vassallo really is today.

"It's about me, my life, my animal friends," he said. "It's about the hopes and dreams of every man and woman who loves and needs to be loved. It's about not letting go and sometimes having to let go. It's about laughing and crying and wanting to return to read, to laugh, to cry again."

Tears and Tales tells of his experiences with rescued animals at Russell's farm, a place always on an island when the creek has filled its banks after a big rain. A few summers ago, he took a visitor on a tour of his farm to meet his animal friends.

The first introduction was with Red Leader, a 15-year-old fit and beautiful horse who wore a dark fly mask over his eyes. "Red came from the New Jersey Standardbred Association and had won $100,000," said Russell. "He had fractured a bone in his leg, and they kept racing him. He broke down totally." The Vassallos bought Red about ten years before, and it was clear he had been treated poorly and lacked trust in humans. "It took a long time to calm him down. He won't let anyone but me ride him," said Russell.

While the visitor watched on that hot day, Red Leader played by jumping around and rolling on the grass, causing Russell to remark that the horse was "showing off to the visitor."

Then two dark-colored dogs, Spunky and Sweetpea, wiggled their way toward the visitor. "Spunky is part Sharpei and part pit bull," Russell said, "and Sweetpea was one of my stories, and I called her 'Git.' She showed up wretched looking because somebody had taken her pups away." There was another dog that appeared to the Vassallos at one point. It was returned to the owners, but the dog tried to come back later.

There are five other horses living on the Vassallo farm: Diablo and Uno (a father-son), Lonesome Dart, Dusty Dart, and Power Blaster, known through Russell's writing as "Taj." They, like nearly all of the animal friends, were rescued from lives of despair.

That unconditional love is shown when one hears the story of Spooky.

"We have three barn cats, one of whom, Spooky, recently came up crippled so we are nursing her in our basement," said Russell. The couple had put Spooky under a vet's care, who recommended putting it down. This was a no-no for Russell, and he paid the vet about a thousand dollars to do what he could for Spooky. Though Spooky still "can't walk straight," said Russell, "he is doing better." Other cats living with the couple in their house are Boots, rescued out on the road, and Sassy, who was the runt of a litter and almost was destroyed by the first owner.

Russell figures that altogether he and his wife have rescued about eighteen animals during the last two decades. Fighting for the welfare of animals has always been important to Russell.

"As a child, one of my grandfather's dogs bit me behind the ear," he said, "and my grandfather, an old Italian who loved his namesake (young Russell Vassallo), wanted to shoot the dog, but I clung to Queenie's neck and wouldn't let go. He had to forego his plans to kill the dog. I was five then."

These days, Russell walks tall and with more confidence. He casts a shadow of goodwill for both his animal and human friends who, like him, have struggled in life. His books sell and he often meets others and shares his wisdom. Deep inside, Russell Vassallo feels thankful for the love his animal friends and other humans have shown him. He is always ready to open his heart and do likewise.

"Sometimes he just cries as he is putting the words down on paper, and then when he reads them," Virginia Vassallo said about watching her husband write his stories. "He's very emotional about it."

That's likely because he remembers those special moments with Palsy long ago. Those times helped rescue Russell from a difficult life, and now he is returning a favor.

Doug and Sheila Bray

Couple Sows Garden of Caring
with 'The Giving Fields'

When Doug and Sheila Bray bought their property along the Ohio River in Melbourne two years ago, they planned to use the house on the forty acres in northern Kentucky as a place to relax in the summer, enjoy themselves and get some well-deserved rest.

As things turned out for the two, they *are* enjoying themselves—but the part about rest may have to wait.

A large area of their land seemed to beg to be made more useful. The field was flat and fertile, but had some challenges to overcome before it could be cultivated. It had a number of trees, a run-down old house and barn, and part of it had a wetland area that probably couldn't be cultivated at all.

But for the Brays, they were always of a mind-set to make things better, a big reason they had such a good and long-lasting business in the past. They began to talk to each other about a better use of the "big old hayfield," as Sheila called it. Those early conversations became serious and would lead to the couple's gift to others less fortunate.

The land and their dream became a project of kindness, and the couple decided to call it "The Giving Fields." Today, people know The Giving Fields is a place where vegetables are grown, then shipped to the Freestore Foodbank, an agency in the area that delivers food to people experiencing difficult financial times.

And though it is just getting started, The Giving Fields is already providing a huge harvest of fresh vegetables such as broccoli, kale, onions, tomatoes, peppers and the like to send to

Freestore locations in Campbell and Kenton counties. It provides healthy, nutritional food to those in need.

The Brays are doing things the right way and for the benefit of others. Both Doug and Sheila emphasize that they want to provide both fresh and safe vegetable produce.

The Brays see their operation as a fitting way they can give back to the community after being richly blessed in their business career.

For Doug, who grew up on a farm near the small town of Grants Lick, it also is a way to honor his mother, who passed away many years ago. "She was always taking food to people who were sick and visiting people in nursing homes," he said. His father was a driver for the family trucking company when Doug was a child. Like Doug's mother, he had a caring heart, carrying surplus vegetables around in his truck, often giving them away to friends and relatives. The family company treated its employees like family, and that has been a shining example for Doug.

Doug and Sheila began talking about their vegetable project to people in the community in December, 2010. "Doug had a big meeting with community leaders and told them what we wanted to do here. We had about thirty-five (attendees)," Sheila said. "The second meeting, we had twice that many show up, including church leaders." Church leaders were important because they committed to recruit volunteers to work at The Giving Fields.

The couple took trips to North Carolina and Florida to observe other projects, along with a local trip to nearby Boone County where St. Timothy Church was also doing a similar vegetable project.

Whenever Doug spoke to community groups about starting the program, he told them they expected to use smart ways of growing their crops and to do it in a way that will keep The Giving Fields going successfully for many years. To make that happen, the Brays found wise advice, and it quickly began to pay off. An agency called the University of Kentucky Cooperative Extension Office provided valuable information. They donated flowers to attract pollination, and showed them how to use "raised beds" and a special irrigation system to spread organic fertilizer onto the crops.

"Within twenty minutes, we can fertilize and water thirty rows," said Doug. They are also learning better ways to control bugs and other pests, and a plastic covering is used to hold down weeds and keep moisture from escaping. Doing this helps cut the amount of labor needed and creates less mud. "As long as we don't have lightning, we can have harvesting any time here," he said.

As he shows with The Giving Fields, Doug Bray knows how to run a business and use all the resources he can to make it be a success. The most important resources are likely the volunteers that Sheila and he bring to the project. Sheila talked about the variety of the citizens who come on the harvesting nights of Sunday and Wednesday.

"There is an 83-year-old woman who comes faithfully all the time," she said. "There are parents who bring their teenagers to have a good learning experience. We also had a group come from the local boys' club. We have all ages (come) to volunteer and it has worked out well."

The skilled work and materials donated to start and keep the project going show confidence in the Brays' leadership. Much of the work for two parking lots on the property was handled by the trucking company owned by Doug's twin brother, Dallas, and younger brother Roger. Others helped them clean up the rubble of the old house and barn along with the grown up fence line. A new fence was built to keep four-wheelers away. A small but powerful solar panel given by a local company stands near the growing area, supplying energy to charge the electric fences that keep out animal predators. Doug's uncle, Ken Flairty, did much of the ground plowing and Tony Burns, a neighbor, has been a jack-of-all-trades for The Giving Fields, including installing the fence and building a stand for the five beehives and the bees that pollinate the plants.

"The real heroes are all the volunteers," Doug said, modestly.

It is true that volunteer support is important in making the project work well. However, without the care and leadership of Doug and Sheila, it likely would not have happened. The two believed in The Giving Fields idea and did the careful preparation necessary for it to work. David Koester, University of Kentucky farming expert, said, "They have done everything from fund-raising to clearing brush and tying tomatoes."

Regarding their hopes for the future of The Giving Fields, the couple wants the project to belong, in a huge way, to everybody in the area.

"It would make me real happy to see this expanding out as far as it would go, and that we would (eventually) have the community running this garden and taking ownership," Shelia said.

But for now, the Brays will need to stay involved. "We don't think about the number of hours we put in," said Doug. "It's just whatever needs to be done."

This year Doug and Shelia are expanding the garden by fifty per cent and planting three hundred apple trees and two hundred, fifty blueberry bushes. They are working with two other locations in northern Kentucky to set up similar garden projects. In the future, they hope to involve local schools and also provide box gardens for senior citizens living in assisted living facilities.

Would not the world be a better place if all dreamed noble dreams … and then put in the work to achieve them?

Bennie Doggett

A Fighter for Struggling People

Bennie Doggett has always let others know where she stands on things of which she cares deeply. She is a person who courageously takes the side of the "underdogs" in her community, people who are poor, who are battling addictions, and often people who are in trouble with the law.

It hasn't been easy for this attractive African-American woman to do such things. She's met dangerous, even violent persons who are influenced by drugs. Bennie has taken on huge utility companies she believes have treated customers wrongly. She's fought hard to get jobs for the unemployed, and she's held hands with the dying. Through it all, she has made friends and some enemies, and she's gained a lot of respect along the way.

Back in the 1980s, Bennie worked as the social-services coordinator for the Northern Kentucky Community Center, in Covington. She was hired as a social worker even though she had no college training. She had, however, an ability to get things done in an area of town with many needs.

"I received my training from life experiences," she said. Bennie used her creativity and people skills to gain a huge group of clients, in large part because she handed out business cards to just about anybody who looked like they needed help. The clients came, and a 1987 newspaper article in The Kentucky Post said: "Ms. Doggett deals with about 6,500 emergency cases each year and counsels 4,500 clients a year. A lot of 'Miss Bennie's' work is conducted outside of her wide-windowed office."

Miss Bennie has not always gone about her work in a calm, easy manner, at least in her early years of work. She once called a government agency in Frankfort, Kentucky's capital, about a local mother and her eleven children who had their electricity turned off. She threatened to call television cameramen to photograph the shivering family if it was not turned on. The company did, but Bennie realized she needed to soften her approach a little bit.

There were many experiences in her childhood that shaped this special person into the hero she is today. She grew up poor in Cincinnati's West End, where as a child she taught her father to read and followed her mother's example of helping the poor and uneducated around her neighborhood. As she grew older, she got even better at those things.

Here are just a few of the caring acts that are part of Bennie's daily life in her Covington neighborhood: taking clients to the hospital, helping those who can't read or fill out food stamp forms, making sure senior citizens get government food supplies, and counseling young people in trouble to change their behaviors and become good citizens.

A few years ago while spending many long, hard hours of service at the Center, Bennie showed another of her skills. A sharp dresser, she opened her own business—a women's clothing store in downtown Covington.

"Not bragging, but God gave me a talent for being creative and being a good organizer," she said. The business did well, and she kept it going for fourteen years. That is, until so many people came to her for help and advice about their problems, along with her sister becoming ill with cancer. As always, Bennie Doggett didn't turn people down who needed her. She spent a year and a half as her sister's caregiver before her sister died.

Bennie then became an outreach worker for Covington's Eastside while working through the Community Action Center, but decided to retire. That didn't last long. She became an active member of the Ninth Street Baptist Church, and she got busy helping people again. "I came out of retirement," she said, "to volunteer thirty-two hours per week at the Oasis Outreach Center." She's still working there, even as she is caring for an ill relative.

At Oasis, the church does many of the things to help others that Doggett did in her other community service jobs. "The Center has been a blessing," she said. "We want to 'claim back' this corner." It recently has moved outside the church building and now sits proudly in an attractive building on Greenup Street, a place where crime and drugs were once a big problem. The building is filled with nice, donated equipment and furniture. People are having their needs met at the Center, with assistance on their mortgages or rent and some are also receiving some food aid. "We have about twenty volunteers all together, and we're able to help with some job training and with those who are homeless," Bennie said.

Bennie Doggett never seems to rest from being a blessing to those in need. In 2010, this wonderful lady of compassion was inducted into the Kentucky Civil Rights and Human Rights Hall of Fame. Her legacy is recognized there and also in the hearts of thousands of lives she has lifted in northern Kentucky and beyond.

Roy Pullam

Born Poor, Teacher Inspires Rich Lives

Roy Pullam won't ever forget how bad it felt growing up in a very, very poor family. Truth be told, he doesn't *want* to forget because, even in those difficult times, "there was always someone who came along and helped me at just the right time," he recalled.

Roy remembers the pain of his childhood, but also those kindnesses shown by people who cared for him. Those memories, both good and bad, spurred the middle-school teacher to do wonderful acts of caring for the needy of his Henderson community. And his leadership inspired many hundreds of young people in his Junior Optimist Club to do the same.

Roy praised both his parents for the life example they showed, despite them not having much money or worldly goods. "My father couldn't read but he was a story-teller and could do all his math in his head," he said. Then there was his mother. "We (the children) came first. And, if there was anyone sick in the community, she would go visit them," he said. "When she died, it was one of the largest funerals ever in our community."

Roy is now in his mid-sixties and retired from active teaching several years ago. He has no trouble remembering a prayer he uttered as a boy living in the small Kentucky town of Providence, in Webster County, where his mother worked many low-paying jobs because his father was disabled.

"I prayed for something to eat. We were hungry," he said, "and the next day this truck pulled up in front of our house and brought us a basket of food." The timely gift was from the local Providence Missionary Society.

Roy noted that his clothes were given to him by the family's church, and that he "was the poorest kid in the school." Classmates ignored him and his self-esteem was low.

"I often felt shame about the experience," he said. "Other kids thought of me as odd … and I *was* odd."

But as Roy grew older, he had some personal "angels" who helped him, like a man who helped him get a college scholarship. But even with the help, Roy had to hitch-hike to Henderson Community College. Later, he transferred and graduated from Murray State College. A very important person to him was a teacher at his high school, who once came to his rescue when another of his teachers embarrassed him in front of the class, telling him that he shouldn't expect to graduate.

"Mrs. Crowe flew down that hallway to that teacher and told him, 'Don't mess with Roy Pullam. He's mine!'" Roy said. "And I *was* hers. She gave me books and made me recite poetry. She taught me what caring was all about." After graduating from college, Roy said that "Crowe was the first person I went to see. She gave me dreams."

And Roy gave *his* students dreams, too. The Junior Optimist Club at Henderson's North Middle School became the world's largest under his leadership. The good works the students did over many years is amazing. They collected over a hundred-thousand cans of food for the Salvation Army and gathered over eight-thousand coats for disadvantaged people. Thousands of books were sent to Americans in the military, along with giving them phone cards. Thousands of eyeglasses were collected and donated by Roy's students, and a local special-needs school, called the Riverview School, received over a hundred-thousand dollars from the club by doing raffles, fairs, and other activities to raise money. And these are just a few of the things his students did, along with the way they grew as persons.

Roy truly has lived a life that is tied to the betterment of others. Besides inspiring those in his classroom, he helped get the

Henderson Drug Court started—a program effective in helping those fighting drug abuse to restart their lives in a more positive way. He worked with a physician to design a local program to screen for the disease of sickle cell anemia. "A simple test that a lot of people didn't know about," he said. Working through the YMCA, Roy and another man started a class to teach third-graders in Henderson swimming skills—a program that may save lives.

Today, he's involved in a bicycle-repair project that is using the services of local jail inmates, and the bikes are given to poor kids in the area. "The inmates are excited and are doing a tremendous job," he said.

Roy often used his filmmaking skills in the classroom. He produced the anti-drug film, "Fourth Down and Too Far to Go …" and what may be the most impressive project is the six hundred audio-visual tapes of notable Kentuckians around the state he and his students made. Together, they traveled thousands of miles to do the oral-history series, and the tapes are available to be viewed at the Henderson County Public Library. Roy has also helped create positive videos for a local reading organization and the United Way.

Roy said his marriage to Velma in 1972 was "the best thing I've ever done." And although the couple had no children of their own, "She was like a second mother to the students all those years," he said. "On all those long bus trips, she sewed the kids' clothes and stayed up with them all night when they were sick and barfing." Velma continues to stand by her husband and his projects of kindness today. She shares his caring nature.

Karen Denton's son was a student of Roy's, and she expressed her appreciation of him.

"Roy has done so much for all the kids in the school and in the community. He has been a mentor and friend to so many in Henderson County and I appreciate his part in helping my son become the person he is," she said.

Kaylie Hester, a former president of the club, said of her teacher: "I know no one more dedicated or more committed to make our community a better place. He is an inspiration for all."

Mrs. Crowe, if she were still around to see him today, would be so proud of Roy Pullam.

Darlene Snyder
Honoring a Commitment

Darlene remembers falling in love with Mike Snyder when she was seven-years-old. However, he didn't pay much attention to her until they started dating at age sixteen.

Even then, Mike sometimes stood her up.

But in time, Mike "came to his senses," said Darlene, laughing.

It was a rocky way to start a love relationship, but it proved worthwhile because the two now have been happily married for over twenty years. Darlene has remained devoted to her husband even though he suffers from bad health and requires a lot of special care from her. She is a grand example of what it means to keep one's marriage commitment through very tough times.

Nowadays, you're likely to see the two riding their motorcycle on the curvy, rural roads of Madison County near their home in Kirksville. They often must stop along the way to pay attention to Mike's health concerns. They're nearly always well-prepared, for which Darlene can be thanked.

Mike began getting very sick in 1994. He developed pancreatitis and ulcerative colitis, and he also had gall bladder surgery. Despite feeling awful, he toughed it out and continued to work at his job driving heavy machinery for the Madison County Road Department. He didn't stop playing his music, either, which was fun for him and a treat for the people in his community. He regularly appeared at nursing homes and churches where he sang, played the guitar, mandolin, dulcimer and banjo.

But in 2003, Mike's mother died. His father died a year later, and Mike became even more ill. Hospital visits became commonplace. More and more, he leaned on Darlene to support him—and she did. Through surgeries, home recoveries and all times between, Darlene demonstrated her love over and over.

When Mike had surgery involving removal of part of his excretory system, the result was the need for him to frequently go to the bathroom, often twenty to thirty times per day. Sometimes there were "accidents," and while staying at the hospital with Mike, Darlene volunteered to help him with clean-ups, a job normally done by hospital staff. She also gathered up soiled linens and washed them at a local laundry mat, and she acted as a good listener and encourager to her husband.

Darlene remembers how Mike came to a point of severe discouragement during one of the hospital stays.

"It was one of the worst days of our marriage," said Darlene, recalling that the pain and frustration of his illness became almost unbearable for her husband. He begged to be taken home from the hospital, and he threatened to "end it all" with his gun. She did all she could to soothe his anxiety and to keep control of her own emotions. After a nurse gave Mike some medicine to settle him down, Darlene expressed her own held-in feelings.

"After Mike received his medicine and went to sleep, I sat beside him in an uncomfortable chair and cried uncontrollably for hours," she said. Then she walked down to the hospital's chapel and received strength by meditating on her personal religious faith.

When the hospital visits became less frequent, and the couple was in the privacy of their home, Darlene thought hard about what she could do to help Mike feel more comfortable and to deepen their relationship. One idea made sense to her regarding his lonely bathroom time. She would simply bring a chair and join him there, in the bathroom, and use the time to enjoy good conversation. The time would become a positive, growing time of personal bonding.

"When my friends found out I was doing this, they thought it was funny, but sweet," Darlene said.

Mike is unable to work at a regular job today and spends most of his time at home, where he does some of the couple's cooking, helps with household chores, writes songs and plays his music. It's when he feels reasonably well that the couple enjoy their scenic rides on their Yamaha 1300 motorcycle, where Darlene enjoys her hobby, photography, and shares the pictures with her Facebook friends and on her website,

Darlene works in the district court office in Richmond, and she checks on Mike often and is always ready to rush home if there is an urgent situation. She is a published writer, too, and she enjoys church leadership roles. Her first priority is her husband, though. He appreciates her for her tender caregiving.

"Darlene is an ordinary person who has been put into an extraordinary predicament and has faced the challenge with grace and dignity," Mike said.

Truly, Darlene Snyder is a Kentuckian who has time-tested her promise to another person and proved herself one of high character.

And to think … it started way back when she was only seven.

Jim Lyon, Sr.

Disabilities No Match for Judge Lyon

If anyone ever told Jim Lyon he wouldn't amount to much because of his physical disabilities, he didn't listen. The fact that he entered this world with two stubs for arms, one stub for a leg and the "good" leg malformed was not a reason to be unsuccessful in his life and career.

Jim's mother made that clear to him years ago, almost as soon as he was born in 1931. Her early encouragement inspired Jim to become a respected lawyer and politician, who served two terms in Kentucky's General Assembly and became a district and circuit court judge for eastern Kentucky's Lewis and Greenup counties. Jim also had a long and prosperous law practice in his hometown of Raceland, as well as coaching in little league ball programs in his community.

"My mother used to say 'My baby doesn't have any hands and doesn't have any leg, but he has a mind,' and that always sat well with me," he said in a clear and pleasant voice. "I never dwell on the negatives."

Jim was born with the shortened arm limbs—better to be called "stubs" than arms. The right leg did not extend as long as where the knee normally would be, thus an artificial leg was needed. The other leg, with its limitations, was also a challenge for him. Despite these obstacles, Jim's childhood play and social activities were similar to his peers while growing up in his Raceland neighborhood over eighty years ago. With the artificial leg, he ran and played softball and football with the other kids. He occasionally got in fights, often with his brother. That sort of thing did not particularly bother his mother, who wanted young Jim treated like others his age. For that reason, she thought it best for her son to attend a regular school in their local area, not a "special" school.

Jim made good grades, both in elementary and high school. He graduated from Raceland High School in 1949—third in his class. That fall, he started college at the University of Kentucky. Many people at the college helped him by making adjustments so that his disabilities would not hinder his success. He used "hooks' on his arm stubs to help him write, but he often was allowed to have a scribe, or person to write information on paper for him.

"I can't say enough good about UK," he said. "They took care of me and gave me a chance. I just had to do the work."

Jim proudly graduated with a law degree from UK in 1955, then set up his law practice in the town of Greenup, near Raceland. He found that using the hooks in his work was a problem. "I had a lot to do to compete with the other lawyers in town, and using my hooks to do paperwork slowed me down," he said, "so I quit using the hooks and I worked much faster." His business began to grow with the help of his secretary, who later became his wife.

In 1958, at the green age of 27, he stepped out and made a bold move—a move that would be very challenging even to an able-bodied person. He ran for election to Kentucky's General Assembly, representing Greenup County—and won. He had always been interested in politics, but he found that the responsibilities of serving were very big. Lots of people tried to get him to vote their way on issues, and it was hard on Jim.

"There were times I'd be awakened in the middle of the night about an issue. It got to be so demanding that I got boils on my arm stubs at times. I had 'legislative stress,'" he said with a grin.

He survived the difficulties and completed two, two-year terms from 1958 to 1962 while he continued his law practice. In 1960, in the middle of his legislative service, he got married. His wife, Jean, has been his constant and supportive partner, both in their home life and as secretary in the law office.

Jim held local office as circuit court master commissioner from 1962 to 1978, then as district judge into the 1980s. On the day after Christmas, 1986, he suffered a heart attack and recuperated at home for about six months after by-pass surgery. He retired in 1994.

Jim Lyon has a kind heart and giving nature. One feels better just spending a few moments around him. His easy way likely was formed by having the loving support of many friends, his wife and family over many years.

Jim has helped many along the way, too. He remembers his days as a courtroom judge: "I always tried to give people who stood before me a second chance," he said. He told of a man who was guilty of a driving-under-the-influence charge, and how he went "a little easy on him." That decision by the judge worked out well. "Years later, he told me that because of that chance, he turned his life around … quit drinking and got back with his wife." Along with those kind acts, he made it a point not to humiliate those who appeared in court.

In retirement, Jim keeps busy by occasionally helping out his lawyer son, James Lyon, Jr. He follows UK sports, and until a few years ago, drove around town in his car adapted to handle his special physical needs. He also greatly adores his five grandchildren, two from his lawyer son, James Lyon, Jr. living nearby and three more from his physician son, Dr. Benjamin Lyon, who practices in Georgetown, Kentucky.

Everywhere he goes, Jim Lyon Sr. has a sweet smile and engaging personality, uplifting to all. He has proven that dwelling on the positives, keeping a focus on difficult goals, and accepting needed support from others—along with hard work—can turn a person into a true overcomer.

Dale Faughn

Senior Citizen Educator, Poet Lives Young

Dale Faughn often got up at 3:30 a.m. to jog three miles before he went to work. He didn't think that doing that was only for the young.

It didn't matter to Dale, born in 1925, that some think young adults are supposed to be the ones who donate their blood to help others live. In his lifetime, Dale has given more than twenty-eight gallons of his blood—drawn from his slender, 140-pound body. He made it a point to encourage others to do so, too.

Dale taught high school science for over sixty years until he retired in 2011. He collected many awards doing it, and was always attending classes to improve his teaching skills. Dale lives young, and he is proof that one can do much of what they set their mind to do.

His life is quite impressive, and he has touched thousands of people in a positive way. Many of them were the students in his classes at Caldwell County High School, in the western Kentucky town of Princeton. Dale loved his work, and he was good at it. He was voted into both the Kentucky and national teacher Halls of Fame.

He also loves to write poems, ones that people can clearly understand and are encouraging. He has a simple love of words and many rich experiences that make his poetry come to life. His skills as a poet became known all around the state, and in 1986, Dale shared the honor of Kentucky Poet Laureate with Jim Wayne Miller. He often quoted the poetry he wrote in his classroom, making it part of the lesson he taught.

The community has recognized Dale for his work in blood donation, too. He was inducted into the Baxter Donor Hall of Fame for his service. He also won "Citizen of the Year" from the Princeton Kiwanis Club.

"Don't be ordinary," Dale likes to say.

And oh, what interesting, true-life stories about his life he tells. Like the five times in 1958 he made a national TV appearance.

"I didn't tell anyone that I was applying," he said, "but I filled out the papers to be on a TV show called 'The $64,000 Challenge.'" Dale soon heard from the show. "They asked me a lot of questions on the phone about my Bible knowledge, then flew me to New York for the program. Before going, a store here in Princeton stayed open after hours to help me get the right suit to wear."

His family and friends cheered him on, and he performed well on the program by "tying with a very nice lady who really knew her Bible well," he recalled. Both received an eight-thousand dollar consolation prize. "Then, in a written test, she beat me, and, therefore, represented the United States at the World Bible Contest in Israel," he explained.

Dale loved telling stories to his students about living poor in the Depression times of the 1930s. It amazed them to hear that their teacher's father was a sharecropper and was also hired by farmers to work "sun (up) to sun (down)" for 50 cents a day in wages. He liked to tell, also, that he was drafted into the U.S. Marine Corps and took a long train trip to San Diego for basic training soon after he graduated from Eddyville High School, in Lyon County.

"We were poor, and I didn't get to go anywhere until going into the Marine Corps," Dale noted. Working hard in school was an important thing in young Dale's family. "My parents pushed education and I hungered to read and learn."

On the trip to San Diego, he took careful notes as he viewed the countryside. Later, when he returned from being on the famous war battle on the island of Iwo Jima, he wrote a poem about his experience called "I Met the Flag at Iwo Jima." He's never stopped writing verses since then.

After he served his time as a Marine, he attended college at Murray State, in Murray. He received money for his education from the GI Bill, the government's way of saying thanks for the military service. He tried to save as much as he could, however.

Dale grins when he tells of his thrifty living style while there. "My tuition, books and fees were paid," he said. "I was given fifty dollars per month to live on, but since they ran out of dormitory space, Murray State found me a place to stay for seven dollars a month, and I spent one dollar per day to eat, plenty. I had thirteen dollars left at the end of each month after room and board."

Feeling blessed, many years later Dale started a yearly thousand dollar college scholarship award for a deserving student planning to be a teacher.

Dale appreciates the help from others that allows for his success. "If you see a turtle sitting on the top of a fence post," he likes to say, "you can know it did not get there by itself. I am grateful for all those who have helped me along the way."

He admits that much of his good fortune is through the help of his wife Virginia, who lives with him at their farm near Fredonia, outside of Princeton. The couple married in October, 1949. They met when he was a student and she worked as a cashier at Murray State's cafeteria. "There was something about the way she punched my meal ticket," Dale said with a smile.

Virginia accepted the fact that she would be married to a very busy person. "It hasn't been easy for her, as I was away so often while she was home raising our seven children," said Dale. "I couldn't have made it without her cooperation." Six of the seven children were boys, and one chose to be a teacher, too.

Virginia's passion is to minister to the hurting in the community. "If someone is sick, Virginia knows just what to take to them," Dale said. Their interests often aren't the same. Most notable is that he likes to travel and she likes staying around home. "Being different has worked well for us," he said.

Besides jogging and other exercises, Dale gives credit for his good health to being careful with what he takes into his body and, simply, thinking like a young person. He takes vitamins and minerals. He avoids caffeine, alcohol and tobacco. It seems to work. "I don't feel old," he said. "It's not age that makes the big difference, it's the way we perceive age."

One thought that guides him in his everyday activities is to never be satisfied with what he does. He wants to do things the right way. In fact, one of his seven books of poetry is named *Don't Be Ordinary*. "I'm not one who just likes to 'glide through'," he said.

Dale's books of poetry, illustrated by his good friend Ricky Phelps, are ways to show that he is a careful observer of life. He uses his poetry writings to encourage both his students and those outside the classroom. He makes sure that one doesn't have to be an English professor for the poems to make sense.

"I write my poems so that anyone can understand them," he said. In a piece called "Forget the Birthdays," he clearly writes his verses.

My message is simple:
Don't wilt up and die;
Don't cower in slavery
To birthdays gone by.

Dale Faughn simply has never used his age as a way to excuse himself from doing what he loves. He meets life with joy and tackles its obstacles in extraordinary ways. He cares enough about the people around him to send the very best—such as a poem he has written for their birthday rather than a store-bought card.

Dale's message he will someday leave behind goes something like this: Always carve out your own individual niche in life—but do it for the betterment of others.

Don Rose

Helping Veterans Tell Their Stories

It made Don Rose sad when he heard that over a thousand American military veterans die every day. It also made him sad that for most of the veterans, their personal stories would never be heard and recorded for history.

Don, a Marine in the Korean War era in the early 1950s, decided to do something about the situation. He would become the "ear" for their stories. He would seek out many of those veterans and interview them. He began working out of his home in Winchester through several organizations: the Library of Congress Veterans History Project, the American Folklife Center, and the national AARP.

Since 2003, Don and his friend, Richard Doughty, have audio and video taped well over a hundred of Kentucky's oldest servicemen as they shared personal accounts: buddies that were lost, their fears, injuries, and their feeling of homesickness. The history of some of our country's wars would be preserved for future generations to know and appreciate.

The taped sessions are archived, or kept for people to see, at the Clark County Public Library in Winchester, where tapes can be checked out or viewed on site, and the Morehead State University History Department, which also has the recordings.

Clark County Library director Julie Maruskin is amazed by Don's leadership in the project. "The Library of Congress has collected twenty-five thousand interviews from all fifty states over a period from 2000-2005," she said. "So, Don has collected nearly half of one percent of the total interviews received from thousands of volunteers nationwide." Julie also figures that Don spends about thirty-five hours for each interview, if preparation and travel time is included.

At Morehead State, Dr. Yvonne Baldwin, chair of the history department, is also grateful for what Rose has done. "I was amazed at his dedication to the cause, but also by his demeanor," she said. "He simply wants the stories told and wants them to be accessible for future generations."

Don seldom receives any help with the costs of doing the interviews, but he thinks what he spends is tiny compared to the price paid by America's veterans. He often wonders about the need to find a better way to solve disputes between nations.

"In my opinion, war is the worst possible way to solve any disagreement. They just ought to let the leaders of two countries fight it out and save all the trouble for everyone else," he stated, only half kidding.

Despite all of the out-of-pocket expenses, the extra time and the effort Don gives, he has no plans to retire from doing the interviewing, even as he suffered with prostate cancer the last few years. "As long as I have names given to me, I will continue to interview," he said, spoken like a Marine who knows and accepts his mission.

Don enthusiastically volunteers around the Winchester community in other ways, too. In 2005, he and his wife, Janet, taught seven defensive driving classes for the local AARP, an organization for citizens over the age of fifty. The couple spent an average of twelve hours per class including preparation, transportation, and teaching. Don often can be seen driving senior citizens to important appointments such as meetings as far away as Frankfort. They are also helping get AARP chapters started in other central Kentucky towns.

Don serves faithfully on the Honor Guard as a member of the Marine Corps League in Winchester. He also grows a robust vegetable garden that is shared with his elderly neighbors.

Whatever it takes, it seems, is what he'll do when he knows of another in need.

But the greatest passion for Don Rose will always be the regard he has for America's military service members who offered such great sacrifice for America and other countries. It still bothers him that many veterans are dying before they tell their stories, and he knows that despite his best efforts and those of others, some of the country's best accounts of history will be lost.

But for Don Rose, it won't be because he didn't do his part.

Kevin Gunderson

Policeman Survives Shooting
to Make His Mark in City Government

It was a hot Friday afternoon, July 18, 1980, when Officer Kevin Gunderson of the Ashland Police Department was practicing his rounds at the shooting range.

On this day, Kevin was subbing for a buddy who had asked for a day off. Kevin loved being a policeman because of the action and excitement his badge promised him. He liked police work almost as much as he did golf, a game he played a lot and played well. So with confidence and spirit, the twenty-four-old acted quickly when a call came to assist the Boyd County Sheriff Department in arresting a man for not paying child support.

The officers had a good idea it could be a dangerous situation, and they were right. With two partners assisting him, one staying with Kevin while entering a run-down house and the other standing watch outside, things got nasty real fast.

Kevin won't forget the ugliness that happened when the suspect was confronted while in bed. "He asked to see the warrant," Kevin recalled, "and when I did show it, he pulled a gun from under the pillow and shot me in the neck. I shot him at the same time, and I fell down instantly, paralyzed."

Kevin described his instant life change this way: "I went from six-feet, four to four-feet, six."

The criminal was shot two more times by the deputy—but strangely, he was able to walk in handcuffs to the police car.

Some things in life don't seem fair, and since Officer Gunderson took the bullet to his neck over twenty years ago, he has not walked and must use a wheelchair.

But Kevin never thought about quitting on a good life. It has been difficult, but he has more than simply survived his difficulty. He has helped better the lives of thousands in the eastern Kentucky community of Ashland.

Just ask the folks around town, where he has served ten terms as a city commissioner, and now a vice-mayor. He began his terms in 1990, and even became mayor for a while in 2008 when Mayor Steve Gilmore resigned to take another job. Kevin often receives the most votes of all the candidates for the commission race.

He has played a large part in things such as developing a shopping mall and other property on the Ashland riverfront, improving the sewer system, and encouraging a sense of pride in the community. He created a helpful web site to share his ideas and to gather more ideas from citizens. Using his specially-made van, Kevin tries very hard to be out among the people and hear what is important to them. He is a man respected because he is an overcomer—and one who gets things done.

The yearly pay for Kevin's work is only six thousand and five hundred dollars, but the people he serves appreciate him so much that they helped pay for two of his costly vans. Kevin is well aware of the many times others have stepped up to help and encourage him through his many years of service. "I owe them and the police department so much," he said. "They have always supported me through everything."

As bad as Kevin's shooting was, it is amazing how quickly he recovered and began a new job. Only nine months after he suffered the gunshot to the neck, he again was employed by the police department, this time as an emergency dispatcher. "I handled the first 911 call in Ashland," he said. The job was not an easy one because the equipment had to be made special for his physical needs. Police Chief Ron McBride commented that Kevin's attitude was "we're going to make this work."

And it did work. Helped by some good problem-solvers Chief McBride helped find around the area, the wounded policeman handled his new position very well through 1988—and then he felt the gentle, but sure, tug of politics pulling at him.

"I had always been interested in politics and had been helping others run for office, so I decided to give it a try for myself," said Kevin. He ran for Ashland city commissioner in 1989 and won, taking office in 1990, where he remains today. He carries out his daily government duties with high energy.

Admirably, he does this after spending ninety minutes in the morning, because of physical challenges, "just getting ready for the day," he said. By now, Kevin has gotten a lot of practice. "I have now actually spent more time in my life as a wheelchair user than ambulatory (walking)," he said.

Even with Kevin's success at working in local government, he has met some other difficulties having to do with his physical challenges. He fell in 1999 while getting off an airplane. It didn't make life any easier. "I'm a little more paralyzed than I was in 1998," he said.

Ron McBride is not surprised by his friend's courage and positive way of living. "Kevin was a hero *before* he was injured," said McBride. "I believe that if he'd not been injured that his future might have been working for the governor in highway safety."

But seeing his public life today, one would find it hard to see how Kevin Gunderson could be any more productive than he's been for the Ashland community. Down but not out, he's shown what determination and a longing to help others can mean.

Bill Gordon

'Wild Bill' Treats Environment with Gentleness

Bill Gordon lived "green" long before it became the popular thing to do. Being a friend of the environment started for him over sixty years ago, shortly after he was born on Christmas Day in 1945. He learned to love the land and appreciate the critters as he grew up in rural Pennsylvania.

Bill was encouraged by his father's love of fishing, hunting, and sail boating. Like his father, he soon gained an adventurous spirit and a keen desire to learn all he could about wildlife and how to take good care of it. He also developed a need to share his love for nature with others.

Today, the tall and well-built man with a reddish ponytail leads others to a better understanding of nature with his High Adventure Wilderness School. It's a school that moves from place to place, and Gordon puts any money he gets back into making his school better and to teach more of his students. It has as its base five hundred rugged, hilly and beautiful acres of mostly wooded area in Menifee County, just east of the town of Stanton, in Powell County. Gordon does his work without any regular helpers.

He has a busy, full life, as he works part-time for a large bookstore in Lexington, too. At the bookstore or other locations such as regular schools, Gordon spreads the gospel of the outdoors and how to both enjoy and act wisely to preserve it. Called "Wild Bill's Wilderness Workshops," the classes are attended by children and adults. His "hands on" teaching style makes for fun learning. His teaching topics include bats, gardening for kids, bluebirds, screech owls and fire-building.

When groups come to Bill's property in Menifee County, his deep knowledge and ability to act on the "teachable moment" turns the hiking and sight-seeing trips into exciting science, history and geography lessons. A bird appears with an unusual mating call, for example. The shed skin of a particular snake is noticed. Maybe there's an interesting looking mushroom. Is it edible? Wild Bill will know. And he won't lecture, he simply shares a bit of knowledge and, if one is lucky, a little wisdom: "Snakes aren't dangerous unless you attack them," he says. "The average person thinks that a copperhead will chase you down and get after you. Unless they're in my yard, I just let one move on."

Bill talks proudly of the water holes he's dug to attract deer and other wildlife, or the bat homes he's built and hung around the property. He likes to tell visitors about how he has done things to make his land have a balanced ecology and how he's acted to stop erosion, repair logging damage and habitat destruction. He has cleaned up old dump sites and restored logging roads, making thirteen miles of hiking trails in the process. "I want people to enjoy the outdoors," said Bill. He believes these steps will help that happen.

Bill explained how people have treated nature badly. "We've tried to get rid of all predators, which are things we are afraid of and things we don't understand," Bill said. "We've done our best to burn, bury, trap, shoot, cut, bulldoze, poison and run over our world trying to civilize and domesticate our surroundings."

Bill is quite comfortable while working at the bookstore, too, especially when he converses with customers about nature books. His easy personality and intelligence draws others toward him. Gary Cremean, the bookstore manager, commented: "Bill has a way of leaning down toward people as they speak, and he always keeps the customer in mind and he relates well to the children and others who come to the workshops."

Bill has been an educator for most of his life. He taught public school in northeastern Ohio for six years. He mixed plenty of lessons on the environment into his regular classes while working with students from both rural and inner-city areas.

There, he owned a farm and turned it into a modern-day homestead. "We tried our best to live a wholesome, rural life," said Bill. "Many of our friends and neighbors were Amish, and they taught us a lot. We were 'green' and didn't know it because that term wasn't invented yet."

During that period, Bill's family took on the challenge of a sailboat journey that lasted two years. They started in Lake Erie, eventually sailed down the Atlantic Coast past Florida, then to the Bahamas. During the second year, they carried both their two-year and four-month-old daughters on the voyage. And, he has continued his sailing trips even in recent times. "To date, I have sailed more than forty thousand miles in the Atlantic, Carribbean, Gulf of Mexico and Great Lakes," said Bill, who also participated in an eight hundred mile sailing race in the Pacific, ending at Cabo San Lucas.

Today, back on the good earth of his land in Menifee County, Bill is inspired by the adventures of his younger days, but puts most of his energy into taking care of his special habitat and teaching about wildlife and the environment.

You might call him a survivor, too. He experienced ice storms that abused Kentuckians several years ago.

But Bill, unlike most, lived quite normally during the time when many had no electricity and heat. He enjoyed both because he uses his own power generator, sheltered in a small outbuilding near his self-built cottage, and he burns wood in his stove. He doesn't need to call a plumber because he keeps a tank of fresh spring water. He also has a compost toilet, using sawdust rather than water for removing wastes. He is also developing a solar and wind generator system to feed power to his "battery bank." The creative ideas will likely keep flowing freely as he continues living in a natural way.

Rather than buying a lot of things and being rich, Bill would rather care for the earth and teach others that ideal, too. He has become one of the true masters in doing so.

For Wild Bill Gordon, being green has, and always will be, the best way to live.